Alfredo de Palchi

THE FAIRLEIGH DICKINSON UNIVERSITY PRESS SERIES IN ITALIAN STUDIES

General Editor: Dr. Anthony Julian Tamburri,
Dean of the John D. Calandra Italian American Institute

The Fairleigh Dickinson University Press Series in Italian Studies is devoted to the publication of scholarly works on Italian literature, film, history, biography, art, and culture, as well as on intercultural connections, such as Italian-American Studies.

On the Web at http://www.fdu.edu/fdupress

Recent Titles

Giorgio Linguaglossa, *Alfredo de Palchi: The Missing Link in Late Twentieth-Century Italian Poetry* (2020)

Daniela Bini, *Portrait of the Artist and His Mother in Twentieth-Century Italian Culture* (2020)

Cinzia Russi, *Sicilian Elements in Andrea Camilleri's Narrative Language: A Linguistic Analysis* (2020)

Raymond Angelo Belliotti, *Values, Virtues, and Vices, Italian Style: Caesar, Dante, Machiavelli, and Garibaldi* (2020)

Elio Attilio Baldi, *The Author in Criticism: Italo Calvino's Authorial Image in Italy, the United States, and the United Kingdom* (2020)

Patrizia Sambuco, *Transmissions of Memory: Echoes, Traumas, and Nostalgia in Post-World War II Italian Culture* (2018)

Thomas Cragin and Laura A. Salsini (eds.), *Resistance, Heroism, Loss: World War II in Italian Film and Literature* (2018)

Catherine Ramsey-Portolano, *Performing Bodies: Female Illness in Italian Literature and Cinema (1860–1920)* (2018)

Ryan Calabretta-Sajder, *Pasolini's Lasting Impressions: Death, Eros, and Literary Enterprise in the Opus of Pier Paolo Pasolini* (2018)

Robert Pirro, *Motherhood, Fatherland, and Primo Levi: The Hidden Groundwork of Agency in His Auschwitz Writings* (2017)

Theodora D. Patrona, *Return Narratives: Ethnic Space in Late-Twentieth-Century Greek American and Italian American Literature* (2017)

Ursula Fanning, *Italian Women's Autobiographical Writings in the Twentieth Century: Constructing Subjects* (2017)

Gabriella Romani and Jennifer Burns (eds.), *The Formation of a National Audience in Italy, 1750–1890: Readers and Spectators of Italian Culture* (2017)

Lisa Sarti and Michael Subialka (eds.), *Pirandello's Visual Philosophy: Imagination and Thought across Media* (2017)

Elena Borelli, *Giovanni Pascoli, Gabriele D'Annunzio, and the Ethics of Desire: Between Action and Contemplation* (2017)

Gregory M. Pell, *Davide Rondoni: Art in the Movement of Creation* (2016)

Sharon Wood and Erica Moretti (eds.), *Annie Chartres Vivanti: Transnational Politics, Identity, and Culture* (2016)

Flavio G. Conti and Alan R. Perry, *Italian Prisoners of War in Pennsylvania: Allies on the Home Front, 1944–1945* (2016)

Graziella Parati (ed.), *Italy and the Cultural Politics of World War I* (2016)

Susan Amatangelo (ed.), *Italian Women at War: Sisters in Arms from the Unification to the Twentieth Century* (2016)

Alberica Bazzoni, Emma Bond, and Katrin Wehling-Giorgi (eds.), *Goliarda Sapienza in Context: Intertextual Relationships with Italian and European Culture* (2016)

Alfredo de Palchi

The Missing Link in Late Twentieth-Century Italian Poetry

Giorgio Linguaglossa
Translated by Steven Grieco-Rathgeb

FAIRLEIGH DICKINSON UNIVERSITY PRESS
Vancouver • Madison • Teaneck • Wroxton

Published by Fairleigh Dickinson University Press
Copublished by The Rowman & Littlefield Publishing Group, Inc.
4501 Forbes Boulevard, Suite 200, Lanham, Maryland 20706
www.rowman.com

Unit A, Whitacre Mews, 26-34 Stannary Street, London SE11 4AB

Fairleigh Dickinson University Press gratefully acknowledges the support received for scholarly publishing from the Friends of FDU Press.

British Library Cataloguing in Publication Information Available

Library of Congress Cataloging-in-Publication Data

ISBN 978-1-68393-269-7 (cloth : alk. paper)
ISBN 978-1-68393-270-3 (electronic)

♾™ The paper used in this publication meets the minimum requirements of American National Standard for Information Sciences—Permanence of Paper for Printed Library Materials, ANSI/NISO Z39.48-1992.f

Contents

Contents

Foreword

Anthony Julian Tamburri

In this keen examination of Alfredo de Palchi's lyrical *oeuvre*, Giorgio Linguaglossa refers to de Palchi as "the missing link in Italian poetry" in the second half of the twentieth century. While such a definitive and overarching statement might draw attention, de Palchi's work has had and continues to have an indelible impact.

From page one of this study, de Palchi's voice is in constant dialogue with the Italian poets of his time. Linguaglossa gives us a complete picture of the relationship between de Palchi's "asymptomatic" creative paradigm and what was taking place around him. In so doing, Linguaglossa recognizes de Palchi's "exasperated individualism," which was never truly recognized, understood, or accepted by hegemonic factions of Italy's literary establishment.

While the majority of de Palchi's life has been spent outside of Italy, mostly in the United States, he has continued to engage with Italy—in his poetry, in translating Italian poets into English (as far back as the early 1960s for *Poetry* magazine), and for close to fifty years as the co-editor, with Sonia Raiziss, of *Chelsea* magazine, a biannual that ceased publication in 2007. The magazine (Chelsea Editions continues today in book form only) published a significant number of translations of twentieth-century Italian poets. Thus, through *Chelsea* magazine, de Palchi also became a conduit, in his own way: bringing Italian poetry to non-Italian-speaking poetry aficionados in the United States.

These two activities—the writing of his own poems in Italian and the introduction of Italian poetry to the non-Italian speaker—constitute two other reasons that we can categorically recognize de Palchi as a missing link in Italian poetry. It is especially his own verse, written outside the geocultural boundaries that we know as "Italy," which makes this study by Giorgio Linguaglossa all the more important.

Italian creative writing (poetry and fiction) outside of Italy is nothing new. Its existence in the United States dates back as far as 1885. What is new is its recognition as being part of a long-standing practice, a tradition, that we can readily label "Italian." Within the past thirty-plus years, occasional essays and book chapters have appeared about this linguistic-literary phenomenon. But we have not witnessed a concerted effort at recognizing such literature as Italian until approximately fifteen years ago (Luigi Fontanella's *La parola transfuga: scrittori italiani in America* [2003]), since which time a number of books—anthologies and full-length, single-authored studies—have been published that clearly acknowledge the existence of Italian literature produced outside Italy.

As editor of the Italian Studies Series for Fairleigh Dickinson University Press, I am delighted to have this book appear in the series. Its publication speaks volumes to the continued open-mindedness of the Press and its desire to go beyond the conventional.

Chapter One

Alfredo de Palchi's Poetry Between Modern and Postmodern Times

Alfredo de Palchi was born in Legnago, near Verona, Italy, on December 13, 1926. He lived in New York, where he tirelessly devoted himself to disseminating Italian poetry both through the literary review *Chelsea* and the publishing house Chelsea Editions. Now that we can leaf through the Italian volume of collected works produced by this Italian poet living in the United States and edited by the indefatigable Roberto Bertoldo and peruse the even larger American bilingual selection of his work (*Paradigm*, Chelsea Editions, 2013) edited by John Taylor, we can also reflect on de Palchi's poetic achievement with a clear mind and a spirit free of prejudice.

The author of *Paradigm* is surely the most asymptomatic of Italian poets who were active in the second half of the twentieth century. The volume's title appears to hit the mark in that it evokes the "new" and "different" stylistic paradigm discernible in de Palchi's poetry. It is here that we find the root of his stylistic individuality vis-à-vis Italian poetry in the late 1900s and into the present century. His first book, *Sessions with My Analyst*, came out through Arnoldo Mondadori Editore in 1967, thanks to Glauco Cambon and Vittorio Sereni's help. After that, there was nothing: de Palchi's poetry vanished from Italy's mainstream publishing houses. The silence enveloping his work in the country of his birth still needs to be fully understood: Though quite astonishing, it is not so difficult to decipher. From the very first collection which he produced, *The Scorpion's Dark Dance* (published only in 1993), which he scratched into the plaster walls of the cells of the Procida and Civitavecchia penitentiaries, where he was held between spring 1947 and spring 1951, we see how this poet's work is fundamentally different both in terms of style and subject from the Italian poetry of those times. Alien to the literary movements that held sway in those years, alien to both post-Hermeticism and the neorealist poetry written in the years following the end of World War II, de Palchi's

1

poetry could never hope to break upon the narrow horizon of Italy's literary intelligentsia. Moreover, the young poet was additionally regarded with deep suspicion for having chosen, when still a boy, to side with the supporters of the Republic of Salò.

De Palchi's poetry was clearly characterized from the very start by an exasperated individualism and the sense of a predestined life journey, which itself becomes the poetic word. De Palchi's *poète maudit* stance has nothing literary about it: It is not fashioned from books but rather by real life, like the poetry of the great François Villon, who became de Palchi's model and enduring point of reference. Thus, while de Palchi's work was, on the one hand, branded as collaborationist and reactionary, on the other, it was never really understood in his homeland, where poetic issues always had a tendency to morph quickly into issues of political-literary affiliation.

With the simultaneous rise in Italy of the "workshop" type of poetic experimentalism and the Neo-Avant-Garde movement, de Palchi's poetry was increasingly dismissed as "minor" and "irrelevant," and so, it was relegated to a region outside the pale of mainstream literature. In brief, it was exorcised and sidelined. His poetic fate had already been decided and sealed. Forced off the playing field, denied access to the dominant literary factions, his work was gradually removed from the sights of the Italian establishment and, despite the high regard shown to it by figures such as Giuliano Manacorda and Giuliano Forti, forced to eke out its life in a sort of ghetto. Finally, what the Italian poetic establishment found and still today finds incomprehensible and indigestible in de Palchi's particular style and craft is how different these were to what in those years was deemed recognizable in a literary sense. His peculiar "identity," the specific manner in which he makes biography and style converge into a single whole, were eventually branded as extraneous to the homegrown poetic tradition.

De Palchi's work would probably have been more intelligible had it been read in the wider context of European poetry (i.e., as an expression closer to other languages and literary traditions). Let us say, euphemistically, that his crafted item was "objectively" off-putting and indigestible to the literary circles of those years. I do not affirm that de Palchi's poetry is superior to, say, Edoardo Sanguineti's *Laborintus* or Pier Paolo Pasolini's *Le ceneri di Gramsci*, or, for that matter, to Paolo Volponi's "ditties" then in vogue; I am just saying that he was also different from and at loggerheads with the decorative mannerism of Sandro Penna's followers and, for that matter, at loggerheads with the Orphic Neo-Mannerists, and the literary taste of the experimentalists on top of that. For this reason, they all objectively and "naturally" shut the doors on the poetry of Alfredo de Palchi.

Today, I believe the time is ripe for us to re-read de Palchi in a new light, free of any prejudice and ideological preconceptions. Reading him in our

present times, we cannot avoid being struck by de Palchi's deeply original poetic path, a path that hails from the "periphery of the world," to quote Joseph
Brodsky, from a geographical and spiritual entity a thousand miles distant
from one's homeland. Indeed, this is a crucial element in his poetry, in fact,
the true element of novelty in 1960s Italian poetry, together with the work
of Amelia Rosselli, who, at that time, was also writing in an unusual style,
one totally unlike the prevailing trend. However, as a result of the battle of
wits then being waged between Pasolini and the nascent Neo-Avant-Garde,
Pasolini, in 1963, published Rosselli's poems in the review *Menabò*, char-
acterizing them as proto-experimentalist, given that they were easier than de
Palchi's to decipher. This, at any rate, was Pasolini's attempted operation.
The Neo-Avant-Garde poets, too, tried to enroll Rosselli among their ranks,
tagging her as an "irregular." De Palchi's work, on the other hand, could
simply not be brought into the fold, both for political and aesthetic reasons.
Thus, it was written off as a literary "mushroom" that resisted any attempt
at classification. To get back to our present day, given that minimalism has
run its course and a "new" critical and poetic sensibility has arisen since the
1990s, we can now recover the historical and aesthetic legitimacy of de Palchi's work and classify it as one of the most important and convincing poetic
experiences that were "sidelined" by Italian poetry in the second half of the
twentieth century.

Chapter Two

The Missing Link in Italian Poetry of the Second Half of the Twentieth Century

Who is Alfredo de Palchi? Is he an Italian poet? Fifty years have gone by since his first book was published in Italy, but leafing through the thousands of poetry almanacs and anthologies published in Italy in the 1960s, nowhere do we find the name de Palchi mentioned. The truth is that de Palchi was a difficult author from the word go. He rebelled against literary "friendships" and was hostile to all compromise and exchanges of courtesies. This was not out of arrogance but rather due to his natural stubbornness vis-à-vis the crisis of literature. Never having had any truck with Italian literature through its official channels, he could afford to be an Italian poet living proudly outside of his country for more than half a century and choose, even more iconoclastically, never to compromise with the mainstream variety of it. To those familiar with the Italian way of doing things, especially in literary circles, this foreign stance of de Palchi's is truly baffling.[1]

Alfredo de Palchi was born in 1926 in Legnano, where he spent his early youth in poverty. Educated up through middle school, he nonetheless stopped his education before getting a degree. As a boy, he had an especially close relationship with his grandfather, who died in 1941 when de Palchi was fifteen; the poet would go on to evoke his grandfather in verse in the 1960s. When World War II began, de Palchi found a job in a workshop and later in a Riello factory. In 1942, de Palchi and his mother moved to Milan, where they lived in a small flat by Piazza San Babila. The following year, with their building having been flattened by bombing when the two were away from home, they moved back to Legnano.

While still a very young man, in a fit of misguided enthusiasm, de Palchi became involved with the Black Brigades. As a result of this association, he was unjustly accused of being part of a murder plot against a Veronese partisan and was brought to trial. Although his lawyer succeeded in proving

5

de Palchi had no part in the crime, nonetheless, he was found guilty and sentenced to life in prison. Eventually, several appeals shortened his sentence, and he left prison in 1951.

But incarceration had the unexpected effect of sparking his career as a poet. As Luigi Fontanella writes, "[E]ven as the experience broke him, it supplied him with the stoic energy he needed to resist, react, read, write and ponder. To mature. And finally to write his peculiar brand of *homme revolté* poetry" (Fontanella 2003). It was in the Poggioreale jail that de Palchi wrote his first poems, scratching them on the bare walls of his cell. Then, at the Procida penitentiary, he met and became a pupil of poet and critic Ennio Contini, who was incarcerated as a political prisoner. Contini spurred the young poet's ambition and guided de Palchi's work for years. It was also in Procida that de Palchi began to read voraciously and systematically, first Italian literature and then French, especially François Villon, Charles Baudelaire, and Arthur Rimbaud. Alessandro Vettori writes of de Palchi's life at this time, "Jail with its closed spaces and lack of freedom, became an apt metaphor for life in general" (Vettori 1997). Some of the gloom of prison doubtless influenced his burgeoning dark poetic tone (Fontanella 2003).

De Palchi's position with regard to both modern culture and official Italian poetry can be compared to that of a rebellious individualist who refuses to view the history of the spirit as a progression developing from *minus* to *maior*, as a type of "enlightenment" that looks to what "lies ahead," to what is more modern and nourishes greater expectations in what the future holds in store. Let us also note that in all his work—from the early 1950s right into the present century—de Palchi left behind the "foundations" that Giovanni Pascoli had laid for Italian poetry in the nineteenth century, and which was to characterize it throughout the following century. De Palchi skips right over both Pascoli and Gabriele D'Annunzio, and so over the whole of nineteenth-century Italian poetry, including the Crepuscolari, who were also linked to Pascoli. To comprehend the youthful de Palchi's rejection of Italian twentieth-century poetry, we need to consider his biographical details—how he got ensnared in a civil war that saw so many of the country's best young people either pulled in on the side of the Republic of Salò or supporting the partisans in their efforts to build a new democratic Italy. We can appreciate de Palchi when we remember his small-town origins—Verona—that he is self-taught and that he acquired his knowledge through his many and passionate readings while in jail. He had a particular penchant for French symbolists like Villon, Rimbaud, Paul Valéry, and Stéphane Mallarmé. He was also interested in Italians, including Giuseppe Ungaretti, Salvatore Quasimodo, Aldo Palazzeschi, Corrado Govoni, and Dino Campana.

This is how de Palchi himself outlines his spiritual and stylistic genealogy in an interview with Roberto Bertoldo, included at the end of this volume:

> It's my taste that rejects the poetry of the Italian nineteenth century and the poetry of the Crepuscolari, not my study of it. . . . Show me the work of one nineteenth-century Italian "poet" who is in any way related to French symbolism. For me that Italian period, up to the very early twentieth century, makes its appearance with weeping willows and trumpets. . . . I appreciate cubist, Dadaist, and surrealist poetry. . . . I totally reject the rancid Italian Neo-Avant-Garde movements of the 1960s. That's ballast, and I say it without regrets. There's enough inanity to make even circus clowns laugh. . . . [A]vant-garde-ness, or originality, is in the text, not in the way you spread the vocabulary across the page amid commas, quotation marks, brackets, etc. (Bertoldo 2008, 5)

De Palchi is part of the generation that spans the 1920s and 1930s and includes such authors as Giancarlo Majorino (1928), Amelia Rosselli (1930), Giovanni Giudici (1924), Andrea Zanzotto (1921), Pier Paolo Pasolini (1922), Elio Pagliarani (1927), Edoardo Sanguineti (1930), and Alfredo Giuliani (1924). Nanni Balestrini (1935) and Antonio Porta (1935) belong to the following generation. You already detect in them the cultural training of the 1960s and 1970s. Between the lines of their work, the crisis of 1968 and the ensuing conservative backlash are both visible. De Palchi has no relation to the events of 1968. Long before that, from autumn 1951 to October 1956, he lived in France and then moved to the United States. Having left Italy for good, de Palchi became a stranger to the events that shaped domestic politics in the country of his birth. He strongly felt the wrench of the civil war and his years in jail. These were the experiences that defined and marked him both psychologically and intellectually. Additionally, we should not underestimate the influence that de Palchi's self-imposed banishment and departure from Italy had on him, for they helped to configure his imagery and fix it at a post-Oedipal stage of growth.

The logical outcome of this was a stylistic fixation as well. De Palchi has no wish to directly control the present. His language and imagery have remained a prisoner to his post-Oedipal and traumatic fixation, at a time, as it were, before history, a mythical age when the I preserves itself in its post-Oedipal fixation and self-replicates in a sort of linguistic self-awareness, revisiting with tragic seriousness the traumas it went through. There is no need for him to experiment with language because his language has become permanently fixed in a sort of historico-Oedipal or rather a pre-historical mold. De Palchi never engaged with neorealism, nor later with the Montale school, nor even later with the Neo-Avant-Garde, because he knew how far removed he was biographically, historically, and stylistically from the developing line of postwar Italian poetry. There was no need for him to come to terms with Italian culture in the 1950s and 1960s. He remained estranged from the places where experimentalism was then being forged: *Officina*, for example, the literary review that ran from 1955 through 1958 under the leadership of Roberto Roversi, Francesco Leonetti, and Pasolini. In the same way, he never felt any attachment to his rural origins in the manner of Zanzotto, who, albeit through the lens of modern twentieth-century experimentalism, saw his native soil protecting him like a mother and giving him the primeval sustenance he required.

Alfonso Berardinelli writes:

> That passion and ideology which led Pasolini to 'experiment' through his 'desperate vitality' of the improvised transcription, could only lead him to the end of all 'styles,' albeit in terms of a personal renunciation and self-disenfranchisement, hounded as he was by his traumas and his private despair. In spite of his literary and cultural limits, which were in the main very typically Italian, resisted mainstream twentieth-century European culture, and remained basically unchanged throughout, Pasolini's creative and intellectual vitality spawned a vast opus: he was a narrator, film director, literary critic (above all with *Passione e ideologia* [1960], and *Descrizioni di descrizioni* [published posthumously in 1979)]) and poet. His poetry—from the mystical-erotic verses in local dialect, *La meglio gioventù* (1954) and *L'usignolo della Chiesa Cattolica* (1958), to the 'civil' poems he penned in the 1950s, *Le ceneri di Gramsci* (1957) and La religione del mio tempo (1961), on to the poem-collages and his articles in verse, *Poesia in forma di rosa* (1964) and *Transumanar e organizzar* (1971)—is a document of his personal and historical trauma. And this is not only down to his outsized narcissism as a writer, but also to Italian democracy's decline, suffocated by the petty conformism of its cultural politics and middle classes.
>
> [. . .]
>
> Zanzotto experimented on a different basis: he rejuvenated the Orphic and Hermetic tradition, gearing his research tools to achieve a molecular dissociation of the units of language, playing at the same time on the highest level of stylistic abstraction, revamping elements gleaned from Petrarch and bucolic and Arcadian sources, and aiming at analytically disassembling language in order to push it to the threshold of aphasia, to single syllabic units and the prattling of children. Here experimentation not only reaches its outer limits, but when Zanzotto successfully pulls off a beautiful poem in carnevalesque and apocalyptic style, he also runs the risk that by exhibiting his workshop, the wonderful linguistic spectacle will collapse into gratuitous and inert monotony. (Berardinelli 1981, 349)

NOTES

1. Two most recent studies on Italians living abroad who write in Italian are Lecomte and Tamburri. Previous work includes: Bonaffini and Perricone; Valesio; Carravetta; and Fontanella.

Chapter Three

The Revolution of Form in the 1950s and 1960s

The Scorpion's Dark Dance

Given the historical, cultural, and biographical details that made him a self-trained intellectual, Alfredo de Palchi quite evidently has nothing in common with the members of the Neo-Avant-Garde and groups like Gruppo 63. Umberto Eco aptly summarizes Renato Poggioli's description of these groups and their approaches to art from *Teoria dell'arte d'avanguardia*:

> . . . activism (fascination with adventure, gratuitousness of the goal), antagonism (to act against something or somebody), nihilism (razing traditional values to the ground), the cult of youth (i.e., the *querelle des anciens et des modernes*), playfulness (art as play), the dominance of poetics over the work, self-propaganda (violently imposing one's own model upon everyone else's), revolutionary-ism and terrorism (in the cultural sense), and finally agonism, understood as the agonistic sense of self-immolation, the capacity for suicide at the right moment, and reveling in one's own catastrophe. Experimentalism, on the other hand, is devotion to the single work. The avant-garde advocates a poetic theory for whose sake it will forsake its own works in favor of producing manifestoes, while experimentalism produces the work and only from the work does it then extract the poetics, or does it allow them to be extracted. (Eco 2003)

De Palchi has no part whatsoever in these Italian cultural debates and the role Marxism played in many of the artistic movements of the day. To understand his poetry, we need to clear our mind of all preconceptions and "unassailable" commonplaces and get familiar with a very different type of poet, with how de Palchi, on the back of his peculiar life experiences, found himself constructing his own artistic individuality as a man who crashed out of Italian history.

In short, we need to see his poetic language as fixed in a time beyond time, a mythical-Oedipal era, outside history, or rather a proto-historical era, deep-frozen in a refrigerator: "refrigerated history." De Palchi's poetic manner is so totally unique that it cannot be likened to any other Italian poetry in the second half of the twentieth century. That peculiar nostalgic distance he has from Italy keeps him well apart from all post-Hermetic and later experimental forms. His language develops in a ripped, intermittent, stylistically twisted manner. It "originates" from the poet's libido, from his phantasmagorias, from the trauma of an unjust prison term that robbed him of six long years of his life. His language is thus dense, nervous, muscular, and clearly repelled by the artificially sweet language of the post-Hermetics. His lexicalism is violent and broken; it exists in a symbolic and iconic universe originating in the poet's ancient fixation with his I traumatized by imprisonment, and this pushes him to forge a psychological-effractive relationship with "objects." In de Palchi's poetry, the I undoubtedly takes center stage, but it is equally off-center and psychologically protective, thus at total loggerheads with the I of the Italian experimentalists.

But there was another poet, four years younger than de Palchi, who wrote in nearly unrecognizable Italian, Amelia Rosselli, whose first poetry collection, *Variazioni belliche*, came out in 1963. Her language, also, seems fixed in a sort of libidinal traumatic immobility, lurching forward with jolts and memory lapses, metrical and syntactical inconsistencies, thick with nonsense and senseless phrasal racking of brains. Her poetry is as unrecognizable as de Palchi's, but it achieved notoriety also because Pier Paolo Pasolini launched her in the literary magazine *Menabò*. Indeed, postwar Italian poetry was then still in some ways dependent on the "framework" provided by Giovanni Pascoli's metrics. Post-Hermetic language was to reach as far into the future as Vittorio Sereni's *Gli immediati dintorni* (1962) and his *Gli strumenti umani* published in 1965. Pascoli's legacy was a template that endured right up to Pasolini, who extracted its last strength in style and language in his *Le ceneri di Gramsci* (1957), where we see Pascoli's high-flown *terzina* attired in a new plebeian, popular vocabulary.

In *La cultura del 900*, Alfonso Berardinelli writes:

> The crisis of the Neo-Avant-Garde, which started in 1968 and lasted into the 70s, is not so much due to the ideological divisions or the success of an alleged literary "restoration," as it is to the fact that Italy's progress towards an "advanced" phase of capitalism had stalled, and now the Italian "crisis" was beginning to rear its ugly head. The increasingly obvious fragmentation of the experience of culture as such, and the changed class identity of the so-called intellectuals diminished the very credibility of a literary battle's existence, and of the working hypothesis the Neo-Avant-Garde had based its action on; i.e., that culture would continue to develop. (Berardinelli 1981, 352–53)

In retrospect, a certain "experimentalism" which, for various reasons, went unnoticed at that time, seems today more meaningful than the positions of the Neo-Avant-Garde movement. I am thinking here of the poetry of Ennio Flaiano in the 1950s, of Rosselli, and of de Palchi in the late 1950s and early 1960s. All maintained features closely linked to their real-life, existential experiences. Today, with sufficient critical distance, we can say that de Palchi's work appears, stylistically speaking, to have more significance and originality than experimentalism, also when seen in the context of modernistic developments in European poetry.

The following are three examples of how the official Italian poetry establishment viewed de Palchi's poetry in the 1980s. The first is a section from Luciano Erba's presentation of a selection of ten poems by the poet, which appeared in the 1983 issue of *Almanacco dello specchio*:

> As Alfredo de Palchi has lived and still lives in New York, his status as an outsider could, albeit somewhat roughly, be better termed as off-center. A poet in New York! Yes, but. . . . Even though we are in the 1980s, we still ran the risk of being served up a series of informal writing exercises—and very informal ones, too—from New York. Instead, Alfredo de Palchi's new pieces have immediately allayed our fears. And not only these fears. However, as it would seem reductive and even inappropriate to hurriedly speak of a de Palchi case, all that's left for us to say is that apparently this highly subjective poetry once again seems not to work. We would then need to turn to its primary quality, its being off-center, how it endures deep down yet fails on the surface. While the phrasal structure reveals a renewed interest in form, and the subject matter at times expresses a felicitous relationship with the world of the senses, the pilot fish continues to live in the ocean's lower depths, both attracted to and pushed away by the light, extremely mobile and restless. (Erba 1983)

Erba's circumvoluted syntax and supercilious choice of words shows us how fastidiously and emphatically he distances himself from a poetry he deems "highly subjective" and "unworkable." Another example of total incomprehension comes from Silvio Ramat. His review of *Sessions with My Analyst*, published July 27, 1967, in *Fiera letteraria*, in spite of all the caution and periphrastic tricks, leaves the reader in no doubt as to its basic assessment:

> In short, de Palchi's poetry seems to originate from the acute angle of his mistrust in the virtues of a discourse based on the twentieth century's main lines. This is the reason for the deliberate precariousness of his phrasing, which we might view as courageously experimental if that same wish to experiment did not lead us to think the opposite. Could it be that de Palchi stayed at the 'informal' level because he feared being able to master "form"? (Ramat 1967)

Another glaring example of the trouble experimentalists had in classifying a poetry so distant from their reading experience is the piece Andrea Zanzotto wrote to motivate the Città di San Vito al Tagliamento poetry prize awarded to de Palchi on July 30, 1988. Here, we see Zanzotto struggling to pigeon-hole de Palchi's poetry inside a completely endogenous historical, stylistic, and hermeneutical perspective. He takes comfort in mapping it exclusively within the confines of Italian literature. This is an awkward and misconceived attempt to fit it into the general and all-comprehensive sphere of "experimentalism":

> De Palchi's poetry has its own unique place in the field of postwar [Italian] experimentalism, never bowing to fashions or to the wish of total subversion. Instead, right from the start he achieves his own balance by basing it on his resentful participation in history's movement in these past decades. De Palchi's expression is clear and at the same time acrid and sharp. Generally we note a succinctness that tends to fix its inner sense in single flashes of images. The ensuing rhythms are broken and shaken, almost like a diagram of the poet's inner emotions, but always restrained, in rejection of any emphasis and ostentatious display, or even of the tragic sense. Here we might detect an analogy between de Palchi and other poets, such as Cattafi and Accrocca, belonging to the Lombard school. De Palchi reconnects the violence he unleashes subliminally, or brazenly, in a tacitly American, big-city context (which however mirrors a situation common in our times), to an obscene mistake of nature, whereby a malignant selection process seems to hold sway working not in favor of the fittest (or the most intelligent), as is often said, but of the "shrewdest"—the cynic who in deception wields his treacherous weapon. Besides demonstrating here his interest in human sciences like psychoanalysis and anthropology, [de Palchi] also takes a very ethical position, even as he rejects all ideologies. (Zanzotto 1988)

We see here the trouble Italian literature had in coming to terms with de Palchi's poetry, as it struggled to glimpse a supposed continuity between him and other Italian poets roughly his age, poets like Bartolo Cattafi and Elio Filippo Accrocca who, in fact, are very unlike one another and also have nothing in common with de Palchi himself.

I mentioned that de Palchi's first book, *Sessions with My Analyst*, which brings together the poems he wrote between 1948 and 1966, once and for all consigns to the history books both the traditional tools of Italian poetry as well as its stylistic groundwork. The youthful de Palchi realized, so very far ahead of his time, that the Neo-Avant-Garde revolution dealt with abstract notions of style, and thus, it was linguistic and formal—a mere scratch on the surface. De Palchi's idea was that the new poetry must go hand in hand with a sensitivity to one's real-life experience. He painfully realized how totally different he was from the Neo-Avant-Garde and the experimentalism of the 1960s, whose work he viewed as Petrarchism overhauled and adapted to Italy's new historical conditions. It was clear to him that a deep, unacknowledged link between experimental poetry and the Pascoli-post-Hermetic formed the bedrock of twentieth-century Italian poetry.

And so, the unthinkable happened: de Palchi's post-modern poetic discourse proved far more advanced than the Neo-Avant-Garde. His proto-experimental experimentalism implies an understanding that poetry's correct direction in the present and in the future is exactly the opposite of that. To run the risk of exploring the linguistically unstable path of poetic language in the post-modern age is itself a challenge of complexity, and so is the sense that poetry includes the dark side of real-life experience, in itself the I's psychological substratum. It will be left for future poetry to claim this sizeable, dark legacy of twentieth-century culture. As there no longer exists a reliable structure of being, so there no longer is the concept of a reliable ontology of poetics. This was the youthful de Palchi's prescience, and it pushed him to embrace the notion that the biological individual and the uniqueness of his experience are crucial in developing a truly distinct poetic discourse, one free of cultural fashions, free as well of the Italian cultural establishment's core assumptions. De Palchi did not budge from his psycholinguistic fixation. Indeed, it constitutes both the central motor and the ignition key of his poetic discourse:

> You condemn me
> you crack my bones but can't
> touch what I think of you:
> jealous of my meaning of a neutral
> courage attacked by noxious conical
> bedbugs
>   —me, a rich meal for you insects,
>   beyond the bristling light
>   I crack my fist down
> (*The Scorpion's Dark Dance*, 62)

*

>   I hold a black
> sunflower seed in my hand—
> knowing that the light sinks behind
> the unconscious / but other nebulae etc.
> are advancing
>   and I have this seed
> to transplant as if
> unique in the un-
> known systems
> (*The Scorpion's Dark Dance*, 11)

In *The Work of Art in the Age of Mechanical Reproduction*, Walter Benjamin clearly states the central problem of modern art: the development of technology is in a blind relationship with "sight," that is, with the ability to survey the ontic horizon. He states: "The sight of immediate reality has become an orchid in the land of technology" (Benjamin 1969, 13). And this type of relationship between the new technological quality of the production process and the ability to technically reproduce a product constitutes the seed cell and the "material" root of general processes, even the abstract and "qualitative" processes of art. "Mass reproduction" of artworks seems to have an inferential relationship with the work of art's "fetish character," he says. "Nature" would then have a "second nature" that increasingly distinguishes itself from the first and begets itself from its own womb. This "second nature" is the *emanzipierte Technik*, which emancipates itself from social control, in the same terms in which "Nature" once presented itself. Drawing away from manual labor, experience gets ready to leave its habitual dwelling and the *sub-jectum* (in the term's literal sense of that which is placed underneath) becomes invisible, an anonymous player.

In the modern age's production cycle, a terminal separation between the work function and the "vision" of the finished product has taken place. The more this "moment" becomes "visible," the more the subject's "blind connection" vis-à-vis the object becomes "invisible." The fate of the poetry of "immediacy" and of "visibility" is now sealed: it is fated to un-disappear from the "gaze" and be replaced by "blindness." As the product begins to circulate as merchandise, the weakening of the lived experience crosses the threshold of production and spreads like a disease, finally reaching even the qualitative activity of the production of art. The "real" thus frees itself by degrees, in a progressive escalation, from the vision of the I, yielding itself up in fragments, in shards. *That* immediacy and *that* vision disappear progressively from the perception of the I. The I discovers itself to be displaced, to be "other," and it is no longer recognizable. Thus the decay of immediacy and the vision of the I also characterize the sphere of the object. The result in the practice of art would lead to the disappearance of art's experience of the aura. In the age in which all styles can be reproduced, the serialization of style causes it to plunge down the bottomless hole of stylization.

This is why all post-avant-garde cultural action is doomed to age precociously. In the 1980s and 1990s, poetry increasingly concentrated on the phenomenon of the poet's private life and his everyday routine. Finally, only poets like Rosselli, de Palchi, and Helle Busacca were left: poets speaking of the I as of stolen goods, of an I robbed, split apart, estranged, taken away. Minimalism's running commentary of the "quotidian" in verse form is a completely different matter, for it takes for granted that in mass-media societies poetry can meaningfully exist only if it is becomes part of "communication." From this point onwards, poetry became the communication of the communicable: Everything is worth a comment, thus everything can become poetry. Poetry was in this way downgraded to the status of comment-communication, a mirror surface of mass-media society.

Steering vigorously away from both the symbolist-auratic poetry typical of the early Eugenio Montale and the simplistic "phonetic" and musical style of the traditional Italian lyric wherein the I survives even as both it and the "body" are alienated, de Palchi moves instead toward a poetry of the imaginary, one whose objects are internalized: a non-phonetic, non-musical, non-melodic, non-auratic, phantasmagorical poetry. A similar thing happened in 1960s avant-garde music, with Giacinto Scelsi, John Cage, Luciano Berio, Morton Feldman, and others opening up new horizons in the field of music. However much de Palchi's poetry may seem dominated by the I, it is immediately clear that it is anything but the I's mere mirror image or its optical projection. Rather, it creates a sort of energy field of the I, which then appears as a vital-phantasmagoric entity, a psychokinetic vehicle. De Palchi is the first poet of the second half of the twentieth century who embraces a poetry in which "objects" are rarefied and broken, where the I struggles furiously inside a texture of dis-location, where the I and its objects are externalized, violently forced outwards: a poetry whose internalized, psychologically unstable objects are projected towards the exterior. This pattern is woven into a web of virulent semantic effractions and psychological lines of force existing in precarious balance, a dissymmetrical, unstable, flammable poetry. Even the metrics de Palchi employs are symptomatic of his stylistic choices: a prosody bereft of metrical schemes, more akin to prose, shot through with a "low-class" word usage prone to invective and words that bruise, razor-sharp jabs at the quietly bourgeois poetry of his fellow travelers. In short, the trauma of World War II and the poet's real-life experiences fused with the issues of the new technological revolution knocking at the door.

Conscious of the melting away of the "new" as a category, a fact that deeply affects poetry, de Palchi realizes he must jettison all-embracing, misleading categories such as the "new," the "old," "tradition," and "anti-tradition." The desperate vitality of his poetry incorporates a tremendous psychological force; it has the power of an earthquake. It comes "rolling" down from the mountain top to the psyche's outskirts, bringing with it a great quantity of heterogeneous elements and literary detritus wrenched out along its existential path, a boiling magma, foaming and full of rocks and sand, nuggets and depleted isotopes down the path of experience. Here we find no polished, shiny metals. There is a broken, fragmented admixture of all psychic strata, whether central or lateral, high or low, in the grand style of the prosaic, the private, and the public. All this gets conglomerated into a disposition of masses inhabited by the fragments of experience and emotion.

Here are some examples of de Palchi's quicksilver-like "poetic matter" from "Remembering 1945" in *Sessions with My Analyst*:

> I follow them, they speak, I don't understand
> I look at the houses the streets, people point
> a finger at me
> —you're a killer—
>
> but the truth is millions of men
>
> I feel this guilt
> I see the guilt in the windows in the street
> in the insane eyes
> of man with his cat-like walk;
> in me the noise the volume of guilt grows
> the unreal victim
> the sense became flesh
> walks with me; within me the burden of the victim
> writhes
> next to me the victim equally
> my brother, his mouth torn away
> writhes
> They drag the culprit
> I am the one, and only Meche assumes an innocence
> that does not bear its weight.
>   Pigeons
> desert the square;
> we turn a corner and there's open country, the night
> the house
>   come toward us.
> (*Sessions with My Analyst,* 45)

This is the highest-capacity poetic fuel we have seen since the postwar years: a super, energy-guzzling vehicle without caring a damn for sustainability, spoiling for the final clash with the entropic, rubble-choked versifying of the experimentalists of the 1950s and 1960s, crossing the time span of decades fiercely loyal to its own idea of style, and finally reaching our current period of stylistic and spiritual stagnation ever cheerful in the face of the looming shipwreck. With *Nihil*, and even more forcefully in *The Aesthetics of Equilibrium* and *Eventi terminali*, de Palchi takes up where he left off in his first book, *The Scorpion's Dark Dance*, as though his poetic journey had come full circle. He has finally returned to his starting point.

As mentioned earlier, de Palchi wrote this first collection of poems in the Procida and Civitavecchia prisons between spring 1947 and spring 1951.

This long poem's metrical scheme is based on an irregular, cacophonous, ruptured, accident-prone beat, bristling with sharp acoustic and semantic angles. No hierarchy in the compositional pattern is to be discerned. Hierarchies are always the result of a conscious stylistic choice. The unconscious affords no hierarchies; everything joins the flux of the "deep experience," which surfaces here and there in the conscious mind. A river—the feminine "Adige"—emerges from the archaic unconscious. The "river bank" emerges, as well as the "borders ravines," "dove," "sugar," "mother," "sunflower," "she-birds," "blond breast"—symbols of the mother from the placental and uterine existence, which collide and spark with symbols of the father: "seed," "spit," "weapon," "rooster," "telegraph pole," "beak," etc. Over all and sundry hangs the curse of the "scorpion" who stages the "dark dance" of death, sorcery, and sacrilege. The scorpion symbolizes worldly degeneration, and it is the psychoanalytical symbol of the unhealthy penis that infects and destroys instead of fertilizing and giving life. The spider is a male figure who makes the "spider's web"—"the spider's web blocks uncertainty." "Uncertainty" is the poet's symptomatic and paradigmatic confession of the suspended condition of the symbolic action which, by suppressing the totem, should heal the terrible injury of having taken birth. But the totem is ever-present. It is invulnerable in its absence. It is invulnerable in that it returns. It is the stuff of ghosts. Like all totems, it hides in recesses, in remote corners, among words. It is invincible. It is a hopeless battle, a hand-to-hand struggle with one's own ghosts: "The bellowing wind butts me into the cell." A symbolic, violent, sterile universe heaves into view, bringing death and barrenness with it. The descendant hangs on to the uncertainty of his birth and imagines himself deep inside the "waters" of the placental river:

> They tell me of my dismayed
> origins in these waters: here I am the heir
> the limpid son—and I love the
> ineluctable
> river . . .
> (*The Scorpion's Dark Dance*, 7)

The fledgling poet takes upon himself the task of ensuring the succession of generations, of regenerating and bequeathing the father's "seed" in other "rivers" to produce the species' immortality. These are the dreams and waking fancies of the youthful de Palchi. His poetry feeds in full measure on them; their function is to make the world habitable and to put consciousness in the service of the hesitant I, ready to enter the historical world. De Palchi dreams of a coming regeneration and, going from one dream to the next, writes poems that thrive on jolts and fragments, rebellions against and insubordination to their majesties the totem and history. The collection closes with the I's ecstatic abandon to the "river" of a longed-for and cherished femininity, the femininity of the placental life, where the contradictions and horrors of history are appeased and forgotten: "In the desert vastness of waters."

The fragment feeds on time and nostalgia. The expectation is its metronome, the fuse that gives the spark. But once triggered, the detonation, the explosion will follow. The poet's nostalgia moves back in time to the principle, the principle of all. It is no coincidence that de Palchi starts his collection with the principle of all things, the big bang, the insemination of the egg. This is the starting point of the principle of evil and history's degeneration. At the molecular level of writing, we clearly see the Oedipal matrix that marks out this unconscious framework and yields one of the most fascinating symbolic transfigurations in twentieth-century Italian poetry.

De Palchi was the first Italian poet in his century to use the "fragment" as a basic building block for his poetry, initially in *The Scorpion's Dark Dance* and later in *Sessions with My Analyst*. Although the second collection was published in 1967, it does not include the poems de Palchi wrote between 1947 and 1951 in the penitentiaries of Procida and Civitavecchia, where he was held after being charged with murder and handed a life sentence by a kangaroo court. This searing experience led him to forge the earliest example of the "fragmentary form" in Italian poetry in the second half of the twentieth century. *Sessions with My Analyst*, chronologically de Palchi's second work, came out with Mondadori in 1967 thanks to Vittorio Sereni's help. De Palchi himself excised *The Scorpion's Dark Dance* from this first collection and published it separately with Xenos Books in the United States in 1993.

De Palchi has remarked: "I began writing this poetry in prison when I was twenty. The compact imagery comes back to life in four sections: the agony of adolescence, of war, of incarceration, and the agony of today—the idea of suicide. I owe many thanks to a poet friend of mine and fellow prisoner, Ennio Contini. He was the one who urged me to write, read, produce."

In those four years of despair and creative writing, de Palchi produced *The Scorpion's Dark Dance*, the twentieth century's first and most accomplished example of the dissemination of poetic language and the technique of verse fragmentation as a poetry form.

In later years, Italian poetry ceased going in that direction. There are different reasons for this. Let me sum them up here. The postwar years saw Italian poetry launching stylistic reform on two fronts. One was triggered by Sereni's *Strumenti umani* (1965), Giovanni Raboni's *Le case della Vetra* (1965), and Giovanni Giudici's *La vita in versi* (1965). On the other side, there was Neo-Avant-Garde experimentalism and the work done by the review *Officina* led by Pasolini, Roberto Roversi, and Francesco Leonetti. Both these attempts at reworking the language of poetry sought to assimilate post-Hermeticism by rendering it irrelevant and pushing ahead with the formulation of new "urban" themes, using a vocabulary close to that of the spoken language, with a subdued tone, a narrative style, civil engagement, eschewing connotation in favor of a denotative, referential style. The undertaking proved successful, for it sidelined post-Hermeticism and undoubtedly helped to give Italian poetry new parameters, pushing it towards linguistic models more adapted to the new mass civilization then in the offing. This same approach remained, however, subservient to a linear notion of the structure of poetic composition: essentially, "discontinuity-continuity-break" in relation to a canonical model of linear writing then perceived to be the rule.

It is obvious that this was not going to be the path followed by the youthful de Palchi locked up in jail in Procida and Civitavecchia. There, he constructed a type of "body" poetry, as it is known today, a poetic form based on emotive fragmentism, miles distant from the stylistic paradigms dominant in those years. His poetry was written live, as it were, during the traumatizing experience of incarceration, which dragged on for six years. A poetry that arises out of the poet's clear awareness of the injustice of his sentence, thus erupting volcanically and seismically. His words are splintered and deeply hurt right from the start, drawing on the memory of the "river" of his early years to counter the present condition, which seems to offer no escape.

The same issue is now being raised again but no longer as the emotive fragmentism pioneered by the progenitor Alfredo de Palchi, who published his admirable, earliest book of poems in Italy only in 2001, inside a volume of collected works bearing the highly significant title of *Paradigma*. Today, de Palchi's poetry can be appreciated thanks to that peculiar lyrical and emotive verticalizing and intensifying manner based on the symbolic and iconic fragmentist style, a poetic form that echoes François Villon and Arthur Rimbaud in the context of modernist poetry, with elements relived and revitalized through the poet's intensely personal and traumatic experience in jail.

I have mentioned the fact that an acknowledgment of the progenitor of the emotive fragmentist style (which some poets have started practicing today in Italy) is urgently overdue. After the great success that the minimalist schools of Rome and Milan enjoyed over the past three or four decades, we detect in the more gifted poets today the need to work a drastic change. It is clear that many of these authors want to change course. They question and write their poems with the aim of reformulating poetry in an iconic and post-symbolist manner. There is an awakening among many of the poets who are in their fifties and sixties or even older. As to the younger ones, it is hard to tell. Sometimes one gets the impression that they are dabbling in obsolete forms of poetry, working with well-tested secondhand models.

The following are excerpts from *The Scorpion's Dark Dance*:

> The first cause
> engrafts the nebulous aorta
> and quickens consciousness
> with the abject drop that splits
> the egg
> starting the womb
> fit for affliction
> (*The Scorpion's Dark Dance*, 5)

*

> They tell me of my dismayed
> origins in these waters: here I am the heir
> the limpid son—and I love the
> ineluctable
> river where the intrigues of my time
> adjust
> deep down I observe my island roll
> toward nothingness
>   the age has changed its ardor
>   the eddy its hornet's nest
> and each wants the why of the other:
> you ever the same, I
> going mad
> (*The Scorpion's Dark Dance*, 7)

*

> My ear at the telegraph pole I catch the hum
> the incandescent emergence ever since
> the earliest origins
> have provoked the earth
>   I perceive
> sparks igniting and wherever I'm scattered
> I hear the uproar of beginnings
> (*The Scorpion's Dark Dance*, 9)

*

> I hold a black
> sunflower seed in my hand—
> knowing that the light sinks behind

the unconscious / but other nebulae
are advancing
        and I have this seed
to transplant as if
unique in the un-
known systems
(*The Scorpion's Dark Dance*, 11)

*

In the fluster
of buds and birds
the door thrusts open on the contest
of the rooster's racket
under the tin roof
and the riverbank meets me with machine shops
threshing floors barnyards from which rises
a ripe smoke of manure
        —the pathway reveals
this commotion to me and I hear
a point of light scratching my eyes
(*The Scorpion's Dark Dance*, 15)

*

Summer
propitious fruit   blond breast
heavy with an onrush of sensations
in the bleating of trees the astringent light
collides
upsets it all: the green
green
the sky-sky and the rumble . . .
(*The Scorpion's Dark Dance*, 17)

*

Smokestacks   fertilizer-
works and sugar refineries
barges loaded with gravel and a few cats
flung from the bridge
pervert this slab of river
this Adige
(*The Scorpion's Dark Dance*, 19)

Chapter Four

Poetry as an Expression
of Libidinal Effraction

A Psychoanalytical Investigation of
The Scorpion's Dark Dance

The passage below is taken from one of the poems in *The Scorpion's Dark Dance*, which Alfredo de Palchi wrote while in jail in Procida and Civitavecchia from spring 1947 to spring 1951:

> [. . .] beside itself, insistent, it brakes
> at the light and flakes off—out of my mind
> I persist in doing the scorpion's
> dark dance
> (*The Scorpion's Dark Dance*, 25)

De Palchi wrote to me as follows: "I had put this collection at the beginning of *Sessions with My Analyst*, but before the book went to press I quickly took it out, as I thought it different in style to the others. Possibly—still today I say possibly—I made a huge mistake. *The Scorpion's Dark Dance* went back into the drawer, and I published it in a bilingual edition much later, in 1993, with Xenos Books in the United States. Thus *Sessions with My Analyst* came out with Mondadori in 1967 in the new series, *Il tornasole*, directed by Vittorio Sereni, minus that earlier, highly significant group of poems."

Let's start with the scorpion. Why does this animal figure in the title? Why does de Palchi use this symbolic word as a nerve center for the group of poems he wrote in the Procida and Civitavecchia jails?

The scorpion appeared on the scene about 350 million years ago and today, apparently, defies the laws of evolution, given that its form has undergone no change since then, as if its body had been perfect for its peculiar lifestyle right from the start. Modern zoologists view scorpions as a puzzle: Neither reptile nor insect, they partake of the nature of both. Insect because their bodies are encased in a shell, but reptiles for how they live underground. Symbols of the amphibian world and also a sexual symbol because of their horrific dance.

Significantly, we find the scorpion in ancient pagan cultures. In Egypt, the animal was worshipped in the female form of the goddess Selkhet, a benevolent deity who protected the underground and bestowed miraculous powers on her adepts. Selkhet's high priests were skilled in charming scorpions. Thanks to their expertise, they could lure the animals out of their burrows without getting stung. Still today, in the East, there are those who are able to sustain continuous contact with these fearful creatures.

While the Mayas worshipped the scorpion as a hunting god and symbol of penitence, in ancient Greece, scorpions were the tool Artemis used to avenge an offense. A legend narrates that the goddess, a huntress and protector of wild animals, was slighted by Orion, who was intent on destroying all animals on earth. In punishment, she sent Orion a large scorpion, which gave him a deadly sting in the heel. The grateful Artemis turned the scorpion into a constellation, and because Orion underwent the same stellar fate, since then, the constellation of Orion flees Scorpius.

In the Old and New Testaments, the scorpion represents the enemy, the devil. The Book of Ezekiel lists those who are hostile to the prophet and his divine word as scorpions. Early Christianity adopted the animal as a symbol of heresy and specious dialectics that challenge the dogmas laid down by the Church Fathers. In its quality as an amphibious and negative symbol, the youthful de Palchi borrowed the image of the scorpion to vehicle a poetry of negativity, of effraction, a symbol of rebellion and heresy, betrayal and defeat.

We can say today, in retrospect, that in the 1960s, when Sereni had the book published by Mondadori, Italian cultural circles were not ready for this type of symbolic message. Indeed, those poems were forgotten and their author banished to a sort of limbo of the "tainted" (i.e., those who had been singled out in the past as being different), and thus, they were irreconcilable and indefensible. The fact that de Palchi had joined the Republic of Salò as a seventeen-year-old lad was seen as a mark of shame that stigmatized his poetry as well. This misunderstanding was most unfortunate and unjustified given that de Palchi had, after six years in prison, been fully cleared of all charges relating to the murder discussed above.

These are the facts, or better, they are the run-up to the facts. The way in which the youthful de Palchi accuses and clears himself of the charges at the unconscious level, signifies a return to the "origins," to the child in the Adige River who seeks "purification" in those waters:

> They tell me of my dismayed
> origins in these waters: here I am the heir
> the limpid son—and I love the
> ineluctable

river where the intrigues of my time
adjust

deep down I observe my island roll
toward nothingness
  the age has changed its ardor
  the eddy its hornet's nest
and each wants the why of the other:
you ever the same, I
going mad
(*The Scorpion's Dark Dance*, 7)

Let us underline that this collection is marked by the presence of de Palchi's unconscious, his bruising conflicts, of which we detect significant traces in all of his future poetry: water, the waters of the Adige River, a symbol both of purification and infection; the "sunflower seed," which symbolizes a rebirth and an embryonic consciousness that goes beyond the symbol of fertility and sexual potency; the traitor; and, finally, fire.

In this same early work of de Palchi's, we find the phrase "tree of fire." The symbolic triangle of water-sperm, or seed-fire, is a clear sign of the metonymic transmission belt that connects the various symbols to one another. Psychoanalysis tells us that fire is one of the commonest symbols of the libido, directly linked to the symbol of the penis: the tree, which emits an incendiary power; the stream of libido, which has the mother as a trigger of transmission, condenses and solidifies in the father-totem, the collective father, the homeland that has outrageously surrendered to the lover, the new father who has usurped the place of the first father. Here, a clear metonymic phenomenon occurs: a shift of the symbolic figures. The rebellion of the protagonist in the poems coincides with the youthful Alfredo's political rebellion against the established order represented by the father's betrayal. And the mother? The mother merely stays outside this process, which is only the business of men: the father-totem and his heretical son ("the mother's knuckles beat at the door").

The son—an outlaw, a heretic, and a rebel—can only respond with a typical child's regression, reaching for the weapon of symbolic dejecta, the "spittle" on all the "traitors" who abandoned and betrayed the real father for a new false father:

At the trampling of crosses upon crosses
I spit out centuries of ancient stones
dog-day roads
and the piquant dung of horses sulking

in the hedges of drought

(at the elbow of the Adige I grew up
on guesses, rumors of other cities)

and I spit on the buddies who betrayed me
and inside me on those who may remember
(*The Scorpion's Dark Dance*, 49)

As soon as the libidinal investment in the mother figure is activated, it must suffer the poet's act of repression, as a result of which the symbolic and metonymic transformation into literary expressions cannot play out. Subjected to an extremely powerful libidinal investment, the mother symbol remains blocked and thus inactive at the literary level.

The language of the unconscious is figurative, metaphorical, and metonymic all at once. It speaks by formulating symbols. It is a language made of scraps, Freudian shifts, metonymic deviations, replacements of names and objects, blinding and incomprehensible metaphors; all these respond to the symbolic logic of the unconscious. In *The Scorpion's Dark Dance,* we read:

I hold a black
sunflower seed in my hand—
knowing that the light sinks behind
the unconscious / but other nebulae
are advancing
            and I have this seed
to transplant as if
unique in the un-
known systems
(*The Scorpion's Dark Dance*, 11)

It is a fire that has its origin in the libido, and its blaze signifies love, but it is also the principal tool with which the heretical son suppresses and cuts down the father-totem, thus a fire that destroys. The heretical son knows he must contribute to the I's total self-destruction so that he can then use that fire against the traitors and the cowards. However, at this exact point, censorship and its attendant power of subsequent suppression step in to forbid the direct naming of the ideational drive coming from the depths of the unconscious. Now the son accepts that he is a hapless coward for not having heeded his unconscious drive to go all the way and slay the totem. This is the "truth" that the young poet seeks so strongly: "On the day of defeat I find that truth."

Sigmund Freud writes: "The warmth that is radiated by fire calls up the same sensation that accompanies a state of sexual excitation, and the shape and movements of a flame suggest a phallus in activity" (Freud, 1962). To use the language of the unconscious, for Freud, this is a *ludus* (game- or gladiator-like) struggle of "phallus against phallus." Prometheus stole fire from the gods and gave it to men for them to make use of it: By so doing, he forced them to give up the pleasure they got from that "struggle." But the "acquisition of fire" ("the rooster's golden splash," which symbolically and clearly equates fire with rooster) marks a basic step in the march of civilization and is "a defeat of instinctual life." As de Palchi expresses it: "On the day of defeat I find that truth."

In the light of this symbolic realization, the unconscious claims victory:

> You condemn me
> you crack my bones but can't
> touch what I think of you:
> jealous of my meaning of a neutral
> courage attacked by noxious conical
> bedbugs
>   —me, a rich meal for you insects,
>   beyond the bristling light
>   I crack my fist down
> (*The Scorpion's Dark Dance*, 61)

In another poem, the I's "ejaculations" are contrasted with the "stink of the shithole," the "stench as of the shithole"—the work of a "fraudulent christ."

Jung states that the skin is the page the psyche writes on. For the twenty-something de Palchi who wrote these poems, the blank pages are the surfaces he carves his words on. As a result, the de Palchian style was electrified: Across all of his later work, he was to employ the irregular metrics of the libido's unconscious instinctuality. The blank paper is, then, the analog of the body's skin: Skin and blank paper are, in fact, the symbolic receivers of communication from the libido, the first track on which the libido's invisible energy reaches the visible world.

For Carl Jung, fire and language are both "products of psychic energy, of the libido or mana. [. . .] Speech and fire-making represent primitive man's victory over his brutish unconsciousness and subsequently became powerful magic devices for overcoming the ever-present 'daemonic' forces lurking in the unconscious. Both these applications of libido required attention, concentration, and inner discipline, thereby facilitating a further development of consciousness" (Jung 1956, 165 and 169). Apart from the question of language, the development of consciousness is undoubtedly related to the production of fire. The evolution of civilization is seen as depending on a dis-

Chapter Five

The 1960s

Sessions with My Analyst

The 1960s in Italy were marked by tumultuous creativity in all spheres, and this also affected poetry. Following the experience of *The Scorpion's Dark Dance*, Alfredo de Palchi again set about exploring a poetic style with structural compactness as its backbone: a poetry based on a broken rhythm, with sudden slowdowns and accelerations. As compared to his first collection, *Sessions with My Analyst* shows more self-assurance in terms of construction, albeit with some loss of expressive immediacy. But this constitutes the poet's natural stylistic growth. The 1960s brought down, one after the other, all the "poetry workshop" notions entertained by Pier Paolo Pasolini and his fellow travelers, even as it undid the solutions put forward by the neo-experimentalists. After Andrea Zanzotto's *La beltà* (1968), poets slowly stopped believing that poetry would be saved by the virtues of the signifier, and this hastened experimentalism's terminal crisis, just as new directions were emerging. One was the Milanese poets' "mini canon," another the minimalism of the Rome-Milan school of poetry. It was in these same years that de Palchi's work was branded as totally unrecognizable and exited the Italian literary scene for good.

Italian poetry in the 1970s and 1980s stayed glued to the notion of linear time. This is hard for us to grasp now, given that our times have marked the passage from Isaac Newton's universe to Albert Einstein's, from there on to Hermann Minkowski, and now to quantum mechanics. We are dealing with a scientific revolution which has no precedent in human history, and which began in the 1950s and reached into the 1990s. By contrast, Italian poetry in the 1960s and 1970s stayed exactly where it was: Poets continued to use a linear syntax that followed Galvano Della Volpe's new thinking around a philosophy of language and a literal interpretation of Saussurian linguistics.

We are speaking of a poetry devoted to the occasion, written in diary-style: understated, self-deprecating, skeptical, themeless, utilitarian, and drawing extensively on the poet's private life. The phenomenon of an invasion of "poets of faith," as Alfonso Berardinelli ironically termed them, happened in the mid-1970s: a myriad of poets, bereft of the cultural baggage of their "fathers," adept in social strategies aiming at visibility and the crafting of a customized, personalized hallmark. Poetry was seen as a "brand" to be marketed in competition with other brands. Obviously, de Palchi was totally alien to this social and cultural context: His was the gaze of a man who had chosen self-imposed exile, away from his homeland. The visibility of his poetry was to be permanently marked by this stance. Clear instances of lines of force that are perpendicular and diagonal subject his work to tremendous pressures, strongly contributing to its strong, jerky, disjointed character.

The following was written by the poet in 1964:

Paradigm

The snake's eye is any kind
of god, a hurricane that uncovers
foundations rafters nails
and in its in-spinning spiral sweeps away
everyday life, leaving the most
fecund reality on the ground

This is the cold beautiful snake,
its flat triangular head like
a religious symbol—I love its
hissing as it slithers along, its tongue
swift to strike out-flung objects
and in its eye are stolidly centered
the emotions of one who cannot react

any snake egg contains a compact form
of any man, while the hurricane is the reality
that fashions the foot, the splendid hand—the paradigm.
(*Paradigm* 2013, 275)

It is quite amazing how, in this composition, the youthful de Palchi replaces unilinear, chronometric time with the "inner time" of memory. Through the metallic, splintered language, a new idea appears, that of "poetic time"; clearly, there emerges a new conception of poetry: the "centrifugal force of objects" and the "hurricane" which "is reality." Here we see the dawn of a new way of writing poetry, one that frees itself from that slavery to objects placed neatly in line by Luciano Anceschi's poetic philosophy, which hinges on the concepts of autonomy and heteronomy (Anceschi 1992). In de Palchi, the recognizable "objects" of the poetry of those years, now so far in the past, do not survive; they have undergone the outward spin of reality and given rise to a new "paradigm." "Paradigm" is a key word of de Palchi's poetry and is, in some ways, similar to "hurricane," "the reality that fashions the foot, the splendid hand—the paradigm." The world has changed, and de Palchi takes cognizance of this from his outpost in New York.

The speaker of the poem no longer coincides with the poem's speaker-out: Indeed, the speaker no longer has the key to the meaning; and if ever he did have the key, now he has either lost it, or it has gone missing. De Palchi's poetry is the first sign of this process, which has grown increasingly clear in our time. There is no longer even a measure of truth that needs to be explored or exhibited since both "content" and "truth" have vanished into thin air. De Palchi is convinced that to dissolve means to resolve historical and emotional conflicts, both of which tend toward dispersion and entropy. And this, in itself, is already a solution. That which has been considered in terms of its problematics no longer coincides with what is experienced in the gut. What is problematic cannot offer itself immediately; it is the emotional blockage that cannot be resolved without a dislocation of the poetic form.

Luigi Fontanella writes:

The stability of this non-communication is thus underlined by the scattered fragments and short passages which signify it (or do not signify it), like verbal sobs, SOS signals sent out to a world that seems muffled and impervious to all cries ('harsh sobbing, inner / turmoil—you listen'). In these sudden sobs—like flashes of blinding light—objects, animals, persons, and relics of past and present life appear and disappear: the image of a rabbit whimpering like a child; the recurring picture of a female secretary's crossed legs under the table; a truck clattering down a dusty country road; bursts of fire from machine guns and guns; ambushes; the guerrilla warfare which de Palchi clumsily took part in—all this in a dramatic crescendo, as the memories come crowding in. [. . .] "The urgency of this uninterrupted stream of consciousness blends excellently with the medley of thoughts, judgments, memories, and projections that are gradually laid out, analyzed, and questioned. All this happens in a discourse that is ever fraught, derisive, broken down to a stammer, where the experimental expression with its many departures from the norm (also mirrored in many daring line placements, or in the irregular use of punctuation) are not part of a premeditated metalinguism (which would be completely alien to him), but always in function of the disjointed inner movement, so as to underline the pauses, the sudden tapering, the lightning quick shifts, the powerful ignitions.[1] (Fontanella 2003)

A caustic, anti-Petrarchan, anti-engagé book, out of place and time, inappropriate, unpresentable, politically incorrect; indeed, it was highly incorrect, due to the typical way de Palchi faces up to his real-life experience by nakedly and crudely portraying the events of the Italian civil war without a whiff of political or literary posturing. The issue here is to submit to the reader a poetry that addresses the crucial nodes of Italian history and the poet's own life as well. The book was given a lukewarm reception and deliberately misunderstood as a psychological book, that's all. Italian poetry at that time was grappling with different problems. A new situation had arisen: From Eugenio Montale's *Satura* (1971) and Pasolini's *Transumanar e organizzar* (1971) onwards, Italian poetry had abandoned the public scene and retreated into a private scenario, fashioning "variegated paper boats" in a journalese style (Montale and Pasolini), a stammering, mumbled style delivered in a unilinear, unidirectional, prose-like language, with a syntax based on time as we can check it by the ticking of our watches and space viewed as a proposition.

In short, if we take the date of 1971 for *Satura*'s publication to mark the beginning of Italian poetry's downward descent in the second half of the twentieth century, we can better understand what followed thereafter. We need but to consider that Tomas Tranströmer's first book, *17 Poems*, was published in 1954! The most revolutionary book of European poetry came out in 1954.

Here, in Italy, the only poet we can hold up is the heretic de Palchi, who in 1967 published the revolutionary *Sessions with My Analyst*, thanks to the good offices of the worthy Vittorio Sereni. And yet the collection barely produced a ripple; in fact, it was misunderstood as a book of applied psychology! As a critic, I feel obliged to re-establish the aesthetic truth of the aesthetic facts, and when I affirm that de Palchi is today the greatest living Italian poet, I don't think I am being hyperbolic. In his own way and in a different cultural and political context, de Palchi did for Italy what Tranströmer did for Sweden. De Palchi literally disintegrates the "time factor" in Italian poetry by fixing it to the historical-libidinal stage of his own adolescence, which coincides with crucial years of Italian history, when the civil war, or partisan struggle against the Fascist regime and Nazi occupation, was in full swing. Time does not exist for de Palchi. It dissolved when, as an eighteen-year-old boy, he took a gun in his hands and, for the love of his homeland, joined the wrong side. De Palchi's poetry is timeless. Time became fixed and frozen forever at the moment when, for the first time, the young poet shoots at the "rebels."

The following is from *Sessions with My Analyst*:

[. . .]

(the truck crosses the town
threads a country road
dotted with potholes / ditches at the shoulders
rows of elms /

my back against the metal cab
protected also by comrades pointing rifles
and machineguns at nothing in particular)
—understand, it's a matter of equipment—
(I hold my 91 between my legs)

suddenly
shots and I
    —already in the ditch—
in my first war
action
was helpless. . .
I pissed in my khakis (ditch water
came up to my knees). I fired when
Sergeant Luigi screamed
"release the safety, bastard!" I

    —too late
    It was the last shot—
            from the ditch
to the tarred sky
my eyes squinting
my face to one side

they laughed: "they ran away
                  you shot a hole
                  up the ass-hole of partisans'"

    —understand?
    they were laughing—
while I was not thinking,
no, of preservation.
I sensed it in the ditch—
(*Sessions with My Analyst*, 125–127)

While Tranströmer in Sweden initiated a revolution of poetry adopting "inner time" as a crucial category on which to construct the new form, in Italian poetry, de Palchi was also busy disintegrating time, annihilating and freezing it into his own brand of fixed inner time. While Tranströmer revolutionized poetry in Sweden, in Italy, de Palchi was being purposely misrepresented as a psychological poet, when it was clear that he was not only a psychological poet.

By the end of the 1950s, it was sufficiently clear that the best European poetry was increasingly focusing on the concept of an inner time grafted onto the poetry-form.

Roman Jakobson wrote that "Edgar Allen Poe's *The Raven* is a poem written for mass consumption or, to use Poe's own phrase, a poem created 'for the express purpose of running'; and it did indeed have a great 'run.' In this mass-oriented poetic utterance, as the author well understood, the reported speech of the avian title-hero is the 'pivot upon which the whole structure might turn.' Actually, this message within a message 'produced a sensation,' and readers were reportedly 'haunted by the Nevermore.' The key, afterwards revealed by the writer himself, lies in his bold experimentation with the processes of communication and with its underlying duality: 'the great element of unexpectedness' combined with its very opposite" (Jakobson 1987, 51–52).

We can paraphrase this as follows: For his part, de Palchi always wrote for himself, never addressing anyone other than himself, and this is the secret of his endurance, of the authenticity of his writing. He skipped straight over the short circuit that almost always links inauthentic poetry to its social and political point of reference. This is how his poetry moved beyond its time and reached us.

Another student of de Palchi's poetry, Antonella Zagaroli, surveys these poems' psychological and psychoanalytical implications. Describing the various states of cognition and distress, she outlines de Palchi's path from an initial acceptance of the monotony of everyday life through to the revelations that arrive in the nineteenth session (Zagaroli 2011, 312–14):

> . . . not that I want to be understood, no one
> understands anyone: I want to find the me
> of my innermost self, the why of your 'why'—

Additional testimony of de Palchi's poetry comes from Roberto Bertoldo, who writes:

> The first impression one gets from reading de Palchi's poems is of texts whose emotion is not intellectual, even though the message often is. If the style of de Palchi's poetry is irascible, even choleric....This signifies that de Palchi's assessment of the world is not hermeneutic but sensual, and conditioned by the clash of the poet with his own self, with his own neurosis. If indeed there is an intellectual stance, it is always mediated by emotive richness, and thus by a language that does not distort the vision but amplifies it in its affective connotations. This happens both when the author references himself and when it is the world that comes over live. (Bertoldo 2000, 37)

Bertoldo highlights the allegorical, emotional, and "even polysemous" levels in the poet's writing. Charting his growth as a poet, he notes the early influences of Giuseppe Ungaretti through to the more meditative styles that developed later. And of the predominantly physical, visceral, and sensual power of the poems, he concludes:

> [De Palchi] is compelled to participate and engage. He does not embrace the phenomenal world out of ethical or civil choice, but because he is obliged to. It is, rather, his humility that determines his civil participation, his resistance. And his moralism, too, is never ideological, but arises out of his pained association with evil and with human inanity. Thus when he writes, de Palchi is simply a man crushed by his experience, and his judgments, his representations are primarily shudders of the flesh. (Bertoldo 2000, 41)

NOTES

1. This passage was translated by Steven Grieco-Rathgeb.

Chapter Six

The Ghost and the "Thing" in the Symbolic Order of Alfredo de Palchi's Poetry

In 1923, Sigmund Freud published a critical text, *The Ego and the Id*, in which he substantiates the shift he had in part anticipated in his work *Beyond the Pleasure Principle* from 1920. In this second work, Freud maintains the distinction between the various psychic realms: the unconscious, the preconscious, and the conscious (Freud 1991). Alfredo de Palchi's poetry gives us the first example of a clean split between the I's imaginary function and its symbolic function in the context of language. The phantasmatic "thing" is the motionless engine that guides de Palchi's poetry; his poetry does not acknowledge metalanguage, and this is the difference between his work and that of Italian experimentalism, which instead adopts metalanguage as an overarching linguistic dimension. The "thing" of language, the ultimate word, can only be posited as missing; a language of the "thing" does not exist, just as the vision of Eurydice is for Orpheus not an object (a cause) of desire since it is precisely the "thing" to open that "void" inside existence, where the word offers itself up as a refraction of presence-absence (i.e., it constitutes something like language). For Jacques Lacan, the "thing" (*das Ding*) appears as a sort of "outside" inside language, an object that is impossible since it cannot be said but at the same time marks, in the word, the very economy of all that can said.

As a fictional character, the ghost signals the outer limit of the symbolic order, guarantees and marks off the boundary between the dimension of sense and the dimension of pleasure, between sense and being, between what is subsumed by the laws of meaning and what is peremptorily subjected to the law of "repetition compulsion," in that sort of anaesthetized area of existence which is the death instinct. It is thus inevitable that the ghost Lacan speaks of should be linked to a liminal dimension, like a stage's closed curtain, enshrouding the further reaches of that nothing of the subject's groundlessness, that void of meanings that begets the "thing." Playing on the pun with *desert*, Lacan calls this boundary *désêtre*.

The subject is never where it thinks it is, and this state of bewilderment (*Unheimlichkeit*) turns it into a directionless wanderer ever seeking its proper place. According to Lacan, "Literally, the ego is an object—an object which fills a certain function which we here call the imaginary function" (Lacan 1988, 44). In other words, the I is unconscious, the product of a code structured around imaginary requirements that pertain to the first phases of life, or a trauma which the subject cannot master and which he is not aware of, which alienate him from himself: "The nucleus of the unconscious consists of instinctual representatives which seek to discharge their cathexis; that is to say, it consists of wishful impulses" (Freud 1991, 190). Man emerges in a "primordial soup" mainly comprising words, which come before him, situate him, determine his openness and closure to the world, his historical and social perspective. Thus language cannot be considered first and foremost an instrument of communication but must be assessed as the condition whereby the "real" comes into being. In this sense, de Palchi's poetic language is already at work, almost magically, the moment the "subject" de Palchi emerges from the erasure of language, from the harrowing experience of unjust imprisonment which he experienced as a compensatory reaction, an act to compensate and reject the "real."

The "subject" is imprisoned inside the web prepared by language, which we can now identify as a bodily effect of pleasure-compensation, a fruit of the reactive and impulse-driven stimuli. The process of signification in de Palchi's poetry is quite simply the process in which the signifiers activated by a compensation-rejection circuit pursue each other. "Meaning" is that which spells out the cross-referencing between the signs, which, as mentioned earlier, Lacan identifies as an instance of "desire," a motor that triggers representation (*Vorstellung*), thus the entire set of cognitive processes. Thought and being are undoubtedly linked in a co-belonging since one is the condition of the other. Between presence and absence we find the throbbing unconscious, its manifestation and disappearance between two signifiers, between the presence of one and the absence of the other. The differential logic that shapes this discourse renders the equivalence of the sign with its own I impossible, hence also the bedrock of classical metaphysics (i.e., the principle of identity). The presence/absence dialectic needs to be interpreted as a differential effect, including the "space" that lies "between" two signifiers: This prevents a falling back into the negative ontology that reifies absence and makes it the foundation of presence. Moreover, the "lack" provides the condition of a deferment between signifiers, which brings into existence a radical difference emerging between the two instances of appearing and disappearing.

Borrowed from Freud, the notion of the ghost in Lacan can help us typify de Palchi's poetry in terms of its phantasmatic fixation on a memory imprint that survives in the preconscious. A correlative of the notion of "lack," this appears as that intangible support upon which the subject maintains the threads of its discourse in relation to the inexpressibility as an absolute condition of desire. It lends, so to speak, a figure to the "thing," gives it a narrative structure, a "secondary scene" in which it can appear as the "lost object."

In the ghost, we see the staging of the subject's elision when the "thing" is found lacking—that sort of extreme, as well as unconscious, symbolic-imaginary redress of a structural weakening which occurs at the ontological level and which yields what Lacan calls, in the more general meaning, the "speaking subject." The ghost is thus both an illusion and also the ultimate answer to the *lack* of the "thing" as a foundation for the subject's being. And what we stress here is precisely its scenic aspect, its literary nature, in which the subject is both an observer and a narrator of what can, to all effects, be defined *the narration of its own lack.* The ghost is, in fact, in the final analysis, a phrase. At the linguistic, symbolic level, it appears as a proposition. At the imaginary level, it is a scene appearing in a static manner, recurrently, almost frozen into a single moment repeated time and again.[1]

The ghost represents the fiction that is a prelude to the truth of the subject as the lack of being, a fictional situation through which the beyond of desire can arise—the desire of nothing and the nothing of desire at the same time—which Lacan indicates, on the back of the Freudian notion of the instinct of death, as pleasure.

According to Lacanian algebra, the ghost corresponds to the formula $\$ < >a$; that is, the barred subject in relation to object "a." The ghost—for this is the horizon of the present analysis—hosts on one and the same stage the two faces of language, the pull between what can be said and what can't.

The barred subject is, in Lacan's language, the subject pure and simple, the subject such as it appears inside the formulation of desire.

"Object a," instead, is the name Lacan gives to the "thing" (i.e., the object lost). It represents, or rather, it "indicates," alludes to the loss itself, the constituent lack and the void that remains after the signifier intervenes at the expense of the "thing" (i.e., the signifier's lethal action).

This is how the ghost announces a sort of linguistic shibboleth, the stage upon which the representation approaches the lack.

The I, says Lacan in his reading of the Freudian term *Entwurf* in *The Seminar, Book VII: The Ethics of Psychoanalysis*, is the functioning unconscious: on the one hand, obliterated by the unconscious; on the other, an extension in reality. Basically, it is a need to represent, and it functions in accordance with a dialectic that merges *Wortvorstellung* and *Sachevorstellung* in a process associating language and representation.

Now we can finally understand how this path prompts de Palchi's words to appear in his linguistic self-awareness every time a particularly creative moment leads *Sache* to reconnect with *Wort*, sparking poetry.

In de Palchi's poetic language, the nothing of desire becomes the desire for nothing, as it tirelessly prowls around the traces of some discovery; for if, as the early Lacan asserts—taking his cue from Georg Wilhelm Friedrich Hegel—desire is fundamentally a desire for recognition (i.e., a desire for desire), the negative implies that there is no real *object* of desire but only, as Freud stated, in the "lost object," in the "un-discovered" nothing.

The objects we encounter in the world, whether they be things or objects of desire, share the same structure that shaped the world in which the I comes into being. The constitution of the I is, says Lacan, the matrix of our relationship with it, inasmuch as the jubilant recovery of the mirror image in the mirror experience pays the price to the dimension of what has been experienced, to the anarchic fragmentariness of the fragmented body, which is what we are. This hiatus is what we bring along with us in the world, and it is the surface on which the subject comes into being: what Lacan terms "the subject of the unconscious."

The subject engages this category, inasmuch as there is no such thing as a subject except in the terms, as we shall see, of a talking subject, only etched on the signifier's lips. However, the language dimension comes into play only if that break happens, and this is summed up in Lacan's phrase, "The signifier represents a subject for another signifier."

Thus language bases itself on the level of the constitution of subjectivity and does not encounter an already shaped subject, so to speak. Language lacerates the human being, the "talking being"; and at the same time, it announces the level of being as a lack, a *manque.*

Among the comments which, in recent times, point to a changing awareness in Italy towards de Palchi's work and the question of a paradigm change, let me quote this appraisal by an Italian poet, Claudio Borghi. On the online literary magazine lombradelleparole.wordpress.com, Borghi recently joined a lively debate on the controversial question of the paradigm change that now appears to be taking place in Italian poetry:

> With regard to the fragment, I was pleased to discover de Palchi, whom I didn't know and consider to be a very excellent poet. His true value has not been sufficiently acknowledged at the critical level. His poetry comes off as a set of electrifying fragments dictated by a frenzied and compulsive anxiety, which even in his more recent texts feeds on the inner man lighting up and firing up his writing, giving it a compelling liveliness and intensity. The thrill he experiences as a poet translates into a lightning-fast sequence of almost elusive frames of lived life: these ignite with a very high frequency, like blinding sparks and

are extinguished at the same speed, lingering in the reader's mind as a sort of trauma-induced sense of bewilderment generated by an incurable, ever-unassuaged wound. It is difficult to make sense of this style of writing critically, and this explains, but certainly does not justify, why the critics who shaped the history of [Italian] poetry in the second half of the twentieth century mostly turned a blind eye to it. Like an animal hunted down by the raptor, Alfredo has crossed through the quiet citadel of the poets and authors who calmly ponder over the mystery of existence and the enigma of divine indifference. Over and above the indisputable quality of these texts, with their shine of authenticity and intensity, the problem remains, I feel, of finding a place at the center of a new poetic paradigm for a poet like de Palchi, who, almost by definition, is one of those authors who cannot have disciples nor create a school of literary followers for he remains anchored to a specific, unique, and unrepeatable life experience and literary expression. Indeed, for different reasons, we could make the same case for [Dino] Campana: though he inspired the Hermetic poets, they, however, never, not even in Montale's *Ossi di seppia,* managed to reach his dizzying heights of expression, given Campana's unique inner experience, touching as it did the borderline with mystical dissolution and even madness. How are we going to get out of what I see as a dire impasse—an impasse that hovers between a need for new juices to be injected into the suffocating world of literature (not only Italian literature, given that this year's Nobel literature prize was awarded to an American songwriter and singer) and the contradictions we encounter when we try to liquidate decades of literature, especially decades of Italian literature, in order to concentrate on inner time and the new poetic theory of the fragment? (Borghi 2016)

Here is someone who has stuck his finger in the festering wound. Somebody in Italy has started to reflect on the need for a change of gear, on the need to forge a different assessment of Italian poetry of the second half of the twentieth century. Indeed, after so many years of misapprehension with regard to both a "paradigm change" and the problem of de Palchi's poetry, now we can finally go back to discuss the de Palchian *oeuvre* as well as our pressing need to change poetry's basic tenets.

NOTES

1. See Lacan (2006, 525): "Desire is produced in the beyond of demand, because in linking the subject's life to its conditions, demand prunes it of need. But desire is also excavated in the [area] shy of demand in that, as an unconditional demand for presence and absence, demand evokes the want-to-be in the three figures of the nothing that constitutes the ground for the demand for love, for the hatred that goes so far as to negate the other's being, and for the unspeakableness of what is not known [*s'ignore*] in its request. In this aporia incarnate [. . .] desire asserts itself as an absolute condition."

Chapter Seven

Reading a Poem by Alfredo de Palchi

"(non-communication)"
in Sessions with My Analyst

The poem begins with the word "(non-communication)" in parentheses, and ends with the un-parentheses word "incompleteness." There is a dialogue, but it is totally disjointed, disrupted, de-territorialized, no longer mindful of the laws of syntax. What is the object? We don't know; there are "fragments," "sobbing," a "you listen" appears, but we don't know who is the one who should be listening. Three or four stumbling lines follow, up to ". . . I speak only in fantasy / to the compact emptiness / of the ceiling." The poet is searching for a "why," searching a "why" like a police inspector looks for clues in a murder case. The text is interspersed with bits of explicit and implicit dialogue—implicit enunciations of a mental monologue. There is a "secretary on the phone," but it is not clear whether she is entering into the dialogue or whether she is trying to "cauterize" it, as you would cauterize a bad growth. The dialogue, or rather the monologue, does not seek a meaning; on the contrary, it backs away from meaning with all its strength, it seeks to break free from the link with "meaning," seeks to free itself from the subservience to "meaning" and "void" and also from the "subservience to syntax," from the alien and constraining power of logic—the supreme power of syntax.

It is true that modern poetry and painting more than all other arts lend themselves to the loss of meaning, the going astray of meaning, the takeover of "emptiness," the sense of loss in the face of "emptiness." Classical poetry, until Giacomo Leopardi's 1821 poem "The Infinite," lent itself to only one interpretation; meaning was organic to the very act of reading. With Modernism, something apparently unusual and disturbing began to happen: the poetic text lost its centrality, and it was no longer the seat of meaning; meaning could no longer be found through a single interpretation but became visible through conflicting readings and interpretations. It became visible only through the problematic nature of conflicting angles. Meaning peers through between the signs of the poetic, musical, figurative text, between the "empty" signs; it tries to rise to the surface but pulls back, moves away, tends to hide. The structure of meaning exists solely in the tension between the meaning's appearing and its concealment: Meaning no longer constitutes the discovery of "truth," for there no longer is any "content of truth" that is stable and definitive; on the contrary, we face a content of truth that is unstable, aleatory, effectual, eventual, residual, imaginary. The structure of meaning only occurs through its residual character: the scraps, leftovers, surrogate materials, supplements. This is its distinguishing mark, the sign of its authenticity, or, at any rate, the sign of its authentic provenance—in the sense that it comes from the author. This is the only possible meaning amid the instability of "empty" signs.

Thus an understanding has become prevalent, whereby a poetic, figurative, or musical text will lend itself to a multiplicity of readings and interpretations. The text has become a "signifier structure" crossed through by the multiplicity of readings. In de Palchi, we have, on the other hand, a "dissipative structure," a structure that loses its signs, an "entropic structure," an entropic loss of signifying signs. What is left in the textual reality are signs that have become unreal and entropic.

What we are speaking of here—the eruption of post-experimentalism—becomes quite clear in Italian poetry as early as the 1960s. These are crucial years; they are years in which Italian society turned a very sharp corner. These are also the years of the economic boom: the masses knocking at the door, the lower middle class aspiring to the fruits of affluence and to a stronger political representation. This is when the flood of domestic appliances accomplished the first and only revolution of Italian society since unification: the TV set, the washing machine, the refrigerator, and the automobile. If we read the poem quoted here, which figures in de Palchi's collection *Sessions with My Analyst,* it is clear how the language of poetry had become a battleground for very strong tensions at the textual level, emotive fibrillations, metrical, syntactic, and semantic disconnections. *The Scorpion's Dark Dance*, written from spring 1947 to spring 1951, is powerfully marked by the act of desecration of an uncontrollable gestural expression; the text is the expression of this act of desecration. In the collection that followed, *Sessions with My Analyst*, the loss of sense and the questioning attitude that ensues become a textual, objective fact. In one word, the act of writing has been de-subjectivized.

> (non-communication)
> fragments:
> harsh sobbing, inner

turmoil—you listen
freezing a print of elms river street
on the wall
      —something I've lost—
while I speak only in fantasy
to the compact emptiness
of the ceiling

      what are you saying; dryly
your "why"
crumbles the office
silence
      —the secretary at the telephone…—
outside the door Monday at one
she answers and to me Saturday
at one the doctor…incredible,
what do I know—
the "why" is a stupid
question—
incommunicable,
not even that disturbs me
      —difficult—
           impossible
to extract, it remains
a paleolithic cave, impossible
to cauterize and still your
"why"

I have no guilt
except other complexes
of the Upper Paleolithic—
"what the secretary's doing" is a matter
of loneliness
incompleteness
(*Sessions with My Analyst*, 117–119)

Chapter Eight

The Issue is the Inexpressibility of the Assertorial Order

Alfredo de Palchi's Poetic Discourse

Alfredo de Palchi's poetic discourse is apparently declarative and denotative since the speaker fears that it could be misconstrued by the reader-responder. This is why the speaker, de Palchi, is forced to express himself through a declarative proposition. A declarative phrase is such when it utters with maximum precision the object it refers to. Even a hyperbole can conceivably be declarative, as also an insult, as long as these refer directly to an object in an immediate and direct manner. Thus, declarative in that it is not interlocutory, not ambiguous (in the Empsonian sense of poetic language's inherent ambiguity); in fact, declarative in the literal sense, in that it avoids the figurative out of a mistrust for the denotative qualities of a figurative discourse.

The declarative style guarantees the assertorial order. And the assertorial order rules out the inexpressible from the logos. The declarative style and the assertorial order are like Siamese twins. But there is a third reject: the unsayable, which returns with the return of the memory footprint and confounds the declarative-denotative style.

De Palchi opts for a declarative discourse, where the speaker orders the discourse in an attempt to avoid the figurative by speaking a word that does not refer to anything different from itself, that does not reference anything implicitly unsaid. But this is an illusion. Even between the seams of declarative-denotative expressions, the nonliteral seeps in, and the figurative brings with it the repressed. The repressed is there as long as it wants to conceal the "other," the "outsider." Just as there is no hierarchy between the literal and the figurative, so a different set of problems comes into being according to whether the pressure is exerted on literalization or, conversely, on de-literalization. It is the problematic nature of the logos which forms the basis of semantic ambiguity; thus, not the signifier that is uncoupled from a subject but rather the signifier for a subject which, in its turn, relates to another signifier. In a certain sense, it is as if the "subject" de Palchi were continuously losing touch with the signifiers and thus also with the signified. This would, for example, explain the improper and forced use of verbs in his poetry.

It is the theme of the "other" and the "outsider" that raises the question we need to ask: whether "the place I occupy as the subject of the signifier is concentric or eccentric in relation to my place as a subject of the signified"[1] (Lacan 1964, 283). Lacan's answer is that the place of the subject is radically eccentric inasmuch as it comes into being as the field of the "other." As the locus of the differential chain of signifiers, the subject comes into being with the signifier, thus is divided. The subject that appears as a result of the other is always an alienated, separate, split subject. We find an analogous structure in Martin Heidegger, where *Ereignis* (the appropriating event) is, concurrently and indissociably, also an *Enteignis* (expropriation). The "other" in Lacan is, first and foremost, the "other" of language as a chain of signifiers, as for Heidegger, language is the "house of being" and the "*Ereignen*'s most appropriate mode"; thus, the selfsame place in which the mutual appropriation of man and being takes place. This relationship bases itself on language's priority and autonomy in relation to man. As Heidegger states: "language speaks," man is spoken, and man is man inasmuch as he is listening and he corresponds to this language that eludes his grasp. Thus, for Lacan, "it is the world of words that creates the world of things [. . .] Thus man speaks, but it is because the symbol has made him a man"[2] (Lacan 1964, 284).

The text in the declarative style is par excellence a testament, and the speaker must hold strictly to the demands of literalization, precisely to sidestep the ambiguities of the phono-symbolic discourse. The paradox here is that in these texts of de Palchi's, the collections *Nihil*, *The Aesthetics of Equilibrium*, and *Eventi terminali*, *Bellezza versus bruttezza* (written August 1–20, 2016), the speaker uses the apodictic language of testaments, in the manner of a *testamentum*, in which the speaker utters his final wishes; moreover, it is also in a prosaic style that is scratched, soiled, torn, pervaded by internal forces that act to widen and spread apart. The feeling is that the more time goes by, the more the poet's conflict-riven language tends to explode, crackle, erupt in fragments, create geological faults that disarticulate the linguistic continent in every direction.

And here, de Palchi utters his final wishes, speaking without giving the responder a thought, for the latter needs only to accept the testament-like legacy of a word that is seismic and earth-shaken by the wound inflicted on the poet *ab origine*. De Palchi goes back to the engram, the primal wound of being charged with murder by an Italian court, and languishing six years in prison waiting for his criminal record to be cleared. In the fifty years of his life since then, the poet has remained immobilized and earth-shaken by this terrible and traumatizing experience. It is the return of the repressed material that here takes place. A strong desire guides de Palchi's poetic discourse towards a compensation that can never be won. It is a deep engram that returns to the threshold of consciousness and demands a secondary reworking of the ideational representative. Indeed, this is the function of de Palchi's poetic discourse: It is a substitute, a supplement rendered necessary by the original engram, the ideational representative's disguise.

De Palchi's use of verbs in the present tense in his three most recent collections points to this return of the engram, this way in which he again introduces the outsider in every moment of time.

The rupturing violence of de Palchi's vocabulary allows us to detect the psychic investment that has come down from those distant years of unjust imprisonment. De Palchi the subject is a split, divided, violated subject, who reacts with a *restitutio* of linguistic violence. De Palchi the subject experiences desire, inasmuch as "desire is the metonymy of the lack of being"[3] (Lacan 1964, 283). Desire, in its eccentric character, is the expression of this "lack-of-being," this negativity that runs through the subject and prevents him from establishing and being established. I feel this problem is important because it sheds light on de Palchi's poetic process, on its rupturing, frictional, volcanic nature. It is not pacified, in short.

NOTES

1. This passage translated by Steven Grieco-Rathgeb.
2. This passage translated by Steven Grieco-Rathgeb.
3. This passage translated by Steven Grieco-Rathgeb.

Chapter Nine

The Unstable Structure of *Anonymous Constellation*

De Palchi's Poetry from the 1970s to the 1990s

In respect to Italian modernism in the first half of the 1900s, it appears evident that Italian poetry in the second half of the century no longer has a controlled certificate of origin: We are now in a field of poetic styles that contrast with and repel each other. We can no longer speak of a "unified" poetry but of different types of poetry which collide with each other. In addition, between the third person of the narrative discourse and the first person of the poetic discourse, there creeps in a secret and dissimulated competition. The past tense of the bourgeois novel stands in opposition to the past tense of Romantic lyrical poetry, in order to kick it out once and for all from mass readership since it is more reassuring, more believable and verifiable, more easily controlled and assimilated. Moreover, the novel offers the guarantee of a believable narrative for a public of consumers to which the bourgeoisie— and, in the twentieth century, the lower middle class—offer the certificate of veracity.

The ambiguity of the "he/she" in nineteenth-century fiction is opposed by the alleged authenticity of the I in the poetic discourse. In the early twentieth century, Aldo Palazzeschi's *I cavalli bianchi* (1905) and Corrado Govoni's *Armonia in grigio* (1907) endangered an order, a measuring system, a monetary system of style (ruled by the class of shifters between equivalent values and a correspondence between signifier and signified), a system of signs that are and can be directed. Poets such as Marino Moretti, Sergio Corazzini, Guido Gozzano, Carlo Vallini, Govoni, and Palazzeschi realized that bourgeois iconology needed to be desecrated with hefty injections of skeptical and carnivalesque "adaptors." Giovanni Pascoli and Gabriele D'Annunzio still saw art as fun and entertainment. The clown, the acrobat, the buffoonery of Palazzeschi, along with the manikins of Giorgio de Chirico, portray the distance they took from the "liberty" Art Deco style and the *Crepuscolari* (twilight poets). From then on, the showy inflation of style passed over into stylization. This was the first warning of a crisis inside the stylistic system. Hence, the invasion of the "liberty" and "floral" Art Deco style, which proved to be the last homogeneous style in Europe.

The rationality of the bourgeois market and its ethics crept into twentieth-century poetry secretly, osmotically, and demotically. With them came the poet's bad conscience. He became a wage earner, an unemployed man, a clown, and an acrobat. Post-Baudelairian poetry was forced to sign up to an obsessive ritual, a system of signs consolidated and verified by the rationality of a "monetary economy" of style, or then rebel against this by undermining the rationality of rational-relational language.

In Italy, Andrea Zanzotto is the best example of the experimentalist culture which hypercritically assumed the precondition of that culture as an incontrovertible given: that is, the irrationality of non-relational language that aims to detach the signifier from meaning and the signified thing. Camillo Pennati's work is an example of a poet who tries to find a way out by connecting with relational-referential language, and from there to reach a poetic language open to osmosis and double-vision word logic.

Zanzotto's poetic discourse is thus loaded with all the multiplicity of meaning; it hypersecularizes the word "numinous," gives pride of place to the hypercriticism of connotation, the rejection of the *denotatum*, trusts in the dislocation, the shifts, and the dispersion of signs in the universal directional system of "landscape." All of Zanzotto's *oeuvre*, from *Dietro il paesaggio* (1951) through *La beltà* (1968) and to *Sovrimpressioni* (2007), pursues the utopia of the signifier and a "landscape" presumed to be pristine, as the utopia of a pristine signifier, exempt from the dire consequences of the Modern.

Conversely, right from *Non un giorno ma adesso* (1960) to his last, *Autunnale barocco* (1978), and in three collections in between, all published by Einaudi—*Notizie dal diluvio* (1969), *Sinfonietta* (1972), and *Lo splendido violino verde* (1976)—the extraordinary and unregulated stylistic compactness of Angelo Maria Ripellino's verse (1923–1978) appeared with extreme clarity. In his earliest work, the Sicilian poet was already "dirtied with the soot of Mitteleuropa." From here, he went on to construct the most eccentric, brilliant, sulfurous, and anomalous aesthetic devices of the 1960s and 1970s: "a swaggering buffoonery," in his own words. His unrivalled cleverness and linguistic skill, sumptuous with harebrained verbal inefficiency, like Marcel Duchamp's *The Large Glass*, which absolutely crushes the melodious emptiness of experimental poetry; a sound box of unpredictable acoustic and verbal effects remarkable for their novelty and originality.

The best work produced by a poet like Milo De Angelis, *Somiglianze* (1976), though it aims to be a strong reaction to the culture of experimentalism is, if we look deep enough inside the signaling and semantic mechanisms, nothing but "internalized experimentalism," going off the tracks of the bonds of inference and inherence which make up the structure of meaning. In brief, we are dealing here with "upended experimentalism." A word like "destiny" in the poetics of De Angelis is a hybrid because, to a certain extent, it also has its origins in post-experimentalism. The words of poetry inhabit language, while destiny inhabits historical existence: We are speaking here of two different and distinct spheres, which De Angelis' poetry aspires to bring together. This is the real crux: And by mistakenly calling itself "fateful," the work of this poet and his successors will never resolve the problem. That a fanciful and acritical reading of Martin Heidegger can indeed lead to this conclusion should not stop us from saying that the practice and theorization of the word "destiny" simply points to the exasperation of a labored concept. De Angelis' first book bases its poetic language on the emotional and emotive structure of a mental and transmental language shorn of all its links and references to instrumental-relational language. He works hard at clearing relational language of all that is rational. Here is the triumph of the "frontal" word, the "destiny" word, which in his followers becomes a sort of secondary supermodelization of poetic language.

In de Palchi's work, we also encounter the "frontal" word but never the "destiny" word. The destiny of human beings is an "anonymous constellation," a concept that needs to be correlated with the poet's indifference towards any ideology of progress or of any stable and enduring human development; his indifference towards using the signifier in correlation with a literary ideology. The destiny of the poet de Palchi was marked *ab origine,* and nothing will alter it. This is why de Palchi is indifferent to the tragic, the comic, the elegiac, the comedy form in dialogue form. He sees the drama of humankind through the conceptual lens of the "anonymous constellation," analogous to the constellations of cosmic dust, gaseous planets, uninhabited planets, extinguished or active stars that spew out light and venomous gamma rays. This is where de Palchi's style hails from, this conception of the cosmos and human history. In his introduction to *Anonymous Constellation,* Alessandro Vettori writes that this book "follows an evolutionary pattern: it starts with iconic reflections on primordial cosmic life, proceeds to meditations on human history, and ends with statements about the poet himself. Evolution is thus both a theme and a structural element of the collection. But do not expect to find the traditional idea of progress repeated in these pages. De Palchi rejects such a positive construct, whereby a series of incremental, developmental steps perfect creation in the course of time. With bitter irony, he asserts the reverse: that violence levels all creatures and brings them back to their primeval state" (Vettori 1997, xi).

In the preface to the poetry anthology *Come è finita la guerra di Troia non ricordo*, I touched on a significant concept:

> The central issue is no longer a question of language, which hides other issues underneath it. The truth is that we no longer inhabit the problem of language, for language itself is no longer a relevant concept, language has become extraterritorial, rafts of meaning that remain in action as long as they are able to produce signs in keeping with the superfetation of "reality."
>
> Very different authors . . . know or sense that it is no longer possible to heal the faults that the Modern era has sprung in categories such as subject, language, reality, all seen once upon a time as stable. Experimentalism sat atop the reassuring conviction that working with causality and chaos in different types of language and manipulating them in this manner was critically significant. Today this is no longer true. The basic assumptions of this philosophy of art have run out.
>
> All in all, experimentalism was a reassuring pursuit: it put things right and supplied certainties and comforts. In the same way, all the hypotheses of poetics that laid down the law and uttered edicts, crumbled into a heap with the crumbling of the foundations, and deterritorialized language. This nihilism, this "X" rolling towards the periphery, as Nietzsche put it, was none other than the subject that went to pieces at the outer limits of our world view. Indeed, this today appears as naked evidence. (Linguaglossa 2016, 5)

In the 1950s, Italian poetry's metrical standard—i.e., metrics based on the hendecasyllabic line, a legacy handed down by Pascoli and the Hermetics—fell into an irreversible crisis. This situation festered on throughout the 1960s and got worse in the 1970s, with the failure of a reformulation of metrics, vocabulary, and style to give poetry in Italy a new lease of life. Italian poetic language was hard hit by the crisis; it could not find an exit scenario, and by trying to salvage what was left, it turned into a niche language, however austere and noble. Bertolucci in later life with *La capanna Indiana* (1951) and *La camera da letto* (1984) and Mario Luzi with *Al fuoco della controversia* (1978) were the last efforts made by a culture of style that had reached its maturity and was now breathing its last. After this, poetry needed to come to terms with the invasion of the language of broadcasting and the mass media. For sure, de Palchi's disruptive proto-experimentalism proved to be the only successful attempt, together with the extremely different poetry of Ennio Flaiano, to circumnavigate this crisis and take on the changed literary scene with stylistically recognizable linguistic garments. Flaiano worked with the superfetation of commonplaces of literary and advertising language, de Palchi with a poetic style that revolves around its own symbolic center. It would indeed be a problem to speak of metrical units in de Palchi's poetry. The metrical scheme forged by Pascoli had fortunately already run its course by the

1950s, when Pasolini published his *Le ceneri di Gramsci* (1957). After that, a generally acknowledged prosody in Italian poetry ceased to be, and the search began for other solutions that might be metrically compatible with traditional forms. These attempts yielded mixed results and include Sereni's moderate reformist tendencies as well as Edoardo Sanguineti and Zanzotto's revolutions in language and style. Ultimately, Italian poetry lost any recognizable metrical uniformity, thus opening to the phenomenon of different prosodies. The 1970s marked the final overthrow of all traditionally sanctioned schemes in this area. The literary establishment decided to ride the tiger. In 1968, Zanzotto published *La beltà*—the final result of experimentalism. Eugenio Montale, for his part, came out with *Satura* in 1971, the first cornerstone of a new conception of metrics in poetry. In 1972, Helle Busacca appeared on the scene to challenge these experiments and to show that the emperor had no clothes on. Her *Quanti del suicidio* (1972) is based on metrical units that are entirely and totally derived from prose. The line breaks only served to signal that there was no going back.

Some continued to resist, thinking in terms of stable metrical units. Others thought of a pacified poetry, adopting the golden mean, a sort of phronesis of poetry. But these were secondary aspects belonging to poetic epigonism.

Anonymous Constellation came out in 1998, published by Caramanica, in a series edited by Luigi Fontanella and Rodolfo di Blasio. The volume includes a preliminary note dated Paris, 1953. Once again, and as always in the past, de Palchi returns here to his libidinal-effractive fixation, his dimension of a man banished from and cheated by his homeland. And here, he attacks the Italian literary establishment:

> The wind of your poetic art is fat, it fills books with ashes; inside your glossy skulls there's your religion, your social and political status pressing (as for politics, the motive for any further, stealthy mention remains unclear); thought feeds on mists and myths; the heart peels out like a metal toy when wound with the wrong key, the key of appearances—why all the fuss over these ashes that are your mask, a rogue's mask? (de Palchi 1998, 15)

The writing here bristles with a percussive and effractive force, a kinetic energy that diffuses in the liquid state of phrastic polynomials. Experimentalist theory envisages polynomials as phrastic entities supplied with a semantic heteronomy; the metrics serve only to stress and underscore the percussive speed of each syntagma. In de Palchi, on the other hand, each syntagma is freestanding, shut inside itself; it serves to reinforce the semantics of the neighboring syntagmata. The result is a style that redoubles and intensifies, concentrating exclusively on the rapidity and precision of the choice of words, used like objects meant to bruise. To achieve this, even the structure of the variable meter is bent to the demands of the "animosity" being expressed. "Constellation" in the sense of primordial nebula, a constellation of clouds of cosmic dust that will one day give birth to stars and planets. "Constellation" as "a total shipwreck that casts on the surface / no fragments of a life / already elsewhere." History has been skipped in its entirety. History is mere historicality that no longer interests the I:

> The contraption eroding my life
> is the surplus which suits me fine
> conscripted under pressure—
> remember,
> perhaps we'll get to the source of it
> a plot of ground where I'll be my own rash
> inquisitor, no walls
> no laws, everything wide open,
> doors windows the bed,
> where no other scum on two legs shall
> judge me.
> (*Anonymous Constellation*, 47)

Anonymous Constellation appeared thirty-one years before *Sessions with My Analyst*, but de Palchi's poetry remains immobilized, chthonian, frozen in time. A traumatized, traumatic, unstable, subsultory poetry that feeds on its own deep instability and could not exist without it. The metrics too are unstable, strongly unbalanced, alive with dissymmetry and dystaxia, always ready for risk like a "beast at bay rending itself in two . . ."; ". . . that breaks in half against the wall / of my conscience."

Chapter Ten

Regarding *Foemina Tellus*

De Palchi's Poetry from the 1990s into the Twenty-First Century

Apropos of Alfonso Berardinelli's *Casi critici. Dal postmoderno alla mutazione*, I quote the passage "*La poesia italiana alla fine del Novecento.*" Here, the critic refers to the horizon of Italian poetry in the final three decades of the past century:

> On the one hand, poetry, as a literary genre, has become increasingly marginalized, or more simply truly "decadent": hollowed out and culturally impoverished. None of the younger poets have attained a measure of significance on the intellectual or critical level. On the other hand, this marginalization has caused authors of poetry to shut themselves inside a ghetto, a type of "reservation" or micro-community where discussion and in-depth intellectual and critical inquiry no longer seem to constitute a vital or primary interest. [. . .] The fact that for almost twenty years not a single poet was an intellectual, a critic, an essayist, reflecting on the meaning of their pursuit and the context in which they work, has contributed to that aforementioned decadence or weakening of poetry as a literary genre. Critical activity certainly has not vanished, but it has become prevalently administrative and promotional in character, not properly critical in spirit. I am thinking of liner notes and blurbs on book covers or even reviews, almost always impeccably executed, arousing curiosity and yet so self-congratulatory, suggesting that the language of criticism is intent on describing textual objects that are more imaginary and hypothetical than real. Indeed, the description is there: what is lacking is judgment. And this, as can readily be understood, also cheapens the quality of the description, for roughly the same things can be said—and are said—both about an excellent book and an unreadable one. Thus everything vanishes into the unreal. [. . .] Given that literary criticism, as we have noted, has become rather sporadic, or not very reliable and insufficiently focused, basically and quite obviously promotional (supplied by the publishing houses or well-connected friends), even the greater or lesser success of this or that author gives an enduring sense of the casual or arbitrary [. . .] In the period

we are looking at [from 1975 onwards], as also in the preceding decade, very often the promotional expertise and quite simply the doggedness with which the authors of poems offered themselves to publishing houses and readers finally made them appear important, meaningful—a must. The function of criticism was in large part replaced by publishers' policies. So, press offices became more influential than any independent critic could ever hope to be. Not only because the traditional or ideal figure of the 'independent critic' had itself begun to decline, but also because poetry as a literary genre had become marginal in the publishing and cultural world. The best critics increasingly turned away from poetry, or tended to be dismissive of it. [. . .]

The fact is that the two generations of young poets appearing after 1975 were soon overshadowed by the literary qualities and historical authority of a number of older poets who had been lucky enough to appear on the literary scene in less confusing and crowded times. (Berardinelli 2012, 305–6)

Berardinelli names these poets: Dario Bellezza, who published his first collection, *Invettive e licenze*, in 1971, and "Patrizia Cavalli published her first book in 1974, Maurizio Cucchi and Milo De Angelis made their debut in 1976." These are followed by Giuseppe Conte, Valentino Zeichen (then in their forties), with the older poets Giancarlo Majorino, Giovanni Raboni, and Luciano Erba and some younger ones, such as Valerio Magrelli. Berardinelli here is extremely sober in his diagnosis and observations. With regard to Bellezza, Cucchi, Conte, Zeichen, and Magrelli, the critic speaks of "men of faith" and "poets by profession," who have "anxiously applied themselves to building their identity and public image." They needed to make an indirect "apology" for their poetry and turn the writing of poetry into a "trade," "since the authors were now facing a readership that no longer was truly competent [. . .], a 'mass' readership. [. . .] Given that a certain vigilance on the part of the critics was over [. . .], the myth of poetry suddenly came back to life. The figure of the poet and ideologue vanished, and the naive or falsely naive poet of faith was next on the scene" (Berardinelli 2012, 306).

At this point, Berardinelli, probably seized by an understandable sense of dismay and bewilderment, does not extend his analysis to the "new authors" whose luck it was to appear on the poetic scene after 1975, under the protective gaze of the self-styled "older" generation. Nor does Berardinelli venture a forecast, merely citing a series of poets he deems worthy. In his judgment, the end of the avant-garde and political-literary commitment also brought to an end that generation of poets and critics—intellectuals in the full sense of the term—who knew how to combine their critical capabilities with their poetic work, and this fact undoubtedly favored a return to the poetry of salvation and absolutes and also dealt a blow to the development of a new poetry emancipated from the "lyrical" and the petty bourgeois. My personal assessment is that the reasons for this crisis are deeper and more complex.

The diminished visibility of the poetry sector must also be put down to the devaluation of culture in general and to how culture has fared intellectually in the brave new world of the mass media. Indeed, the poetry sector, the weakest link in the cultural world, has most violently and glaringly suffered from the silence of publishers and the media. The phenomenon was historical and social as much as it was aesthetic.

Here, we need to make a distinction. The war for status that appeared over the horizon in the 1980s and 1990s was fought among the poets of the "1975 generation"—the poets of the "small canon," as Berardinelli ironically calls them—and the "new poets," who started publishing after 1975 and suffered marginalization and silence. A startling phenomenon then took place: On one side, we have the "small canon" poets who had the will through publishing and self-promotion to make a name for themselves and so consolidate their hegemony and visibility; on the other side are the "new poets," the generation of fifty-somethings, who never became visible, marginalized as they were by the big publishing houses and forced into a sort of existential and cultural no-man's-land.

A clear instance of this is Maurizio Cucchi and Stefano Giovanardi's *Poeti italiani del secondo Novecento*, published by Mondadori in its Meridiani series. This anthology "consecrates and artificially fixes a situation which, all in all, is quite confused," remarks Berardinelli, and he adds: "The anthology basically sells the truly 'stable' editorial values established in the last two or three decades of the twentieth century. As if nothing new had happened on the literary scene" (Berardinelli 2012, 306). The criterion the two editors used for their anthology—to feature only poets published before 1995 by major publishing houses—is not only questionable and scientifically unreliable, it also resorts to a small trick to sanction the status quo decreed by the strategists of the "small canon": in other words, to set the rules of the game while the game is taking place, and so exclude the generation which, in the preceding two decades, had worked towards a renewal of poetry.

In 1957, in the ninth issue of *Officina*, Pier Paolo Pasolini said this about experimentalism: "Even though they have thrown off the security of a world that is stylistically mature, refined and even dramatic and soulful (which, in any case, we must continue to be users of), not one of the 'official' ideologies wins us over [. . .]." The article goes on to discuss how "experimentation and invention have been rolled into one" (!?) and speaks of a "cultural operation" in which language "is generally lowered straight down to the level of prose, that is, to the rational, the logical, the historical," thus "re-adopting the stylistic modes existing prior to the twentieth century" (Berardinelli 2012, 307).

Fifty years have gone by since these notes were set down, and poetry still seems fixed where Pasolini left off. We have a world that is "stylistically mature," an array of "objects" with full poetic credentials; there is a declarative style that is suitable for presenting these "objects"; there is a lowering of the poetic language to meet "the level of prose." In short, and quite incredibly, we are still at the starting line. There are some who survive in the shade of a "stylistically mature world" and live off the recognition their style affords them, and those who are happy enough to go down already trodden paths, like hunting dogs following in the footsteps of their predecessors, in the wake of a stylistic tradition that lends them a degree of recognizability; and there are those who believe that today the crucial issue is to lower the language of poetry "entirely down to the level of prose." But the question is immeasurably more complex, if only because, meanwhile, the crisis of poetic discourse has only grown worse. Yes, today there is most probably a widespread longing or nostalgia for the long-vanished "stylistically mature world." But like the *Titanic*, this is a tradition that seems instead to have sunk after crashing into the iceberg of modernity.

This fact appears quite obvious: Contemporary poetry has become a poetry of the "everyday," at the same time growing "abstract"; it is a discourse around deliverance and compensation, a poetry for the experts of a super-modelled language. There are those who go on producing gastronomic poetry, an easily communicable and recognizable style that has a certain positive impact on the general readership. But this is a hoax, a false perspective, an optical confusion and a philosophical mistake. The poetry of epigonism may certainly, in the short term, exercise a certain allure, a certain ascendancy; its influence can function amid a circle of initiates and within the confines of a well-oiled institutionalized approach to style. Indeed, this is how hegemonic situations take shape: The ascending line of a stylistic tradition contemplates an immediately recognizable descending line. All the literary products that belong to the descending line are easily recognizable in virtue of the ascending line. This is how a tradition of style comes into being. What Luciano Anceschi in 1952 defined as the "poetry of objects" has today become commonplace, adopted by a mixed bag of imitators: a "poetry of the accumulation of objects," the "rarefying of objects," as if the "objects" per se possessed a mana, a magical ability that allows them to conjure numinous effects on the printed page. As a matter of fact, when "objects" have no objective correlative, they cannot respond to aesthetic communication; they can only produce effects in the sphere of an instrumental, infra-aesthetic communication. This is the radical misunderstanding which, from the 1990s to the present, has snared all attempts undertaken by the poetry of "objects" to make "objects" speak. No effort is made to discuss the fact that "objects" are always "linguistic objects" and that a poetry rich in "objects" is not the same as a poetry rich in "linguistic objects." Thus, those "objects" remain mute; they are signs that lead back to a short-circuited system. During the 1990s, the post-experimental school had clearly exhausted its powers, while the "everyday" poetry of the Lombard school was on its seemingly endless and inconclusive path towards imitation (Berardinelli 2012, 307).

In this context of Italian mainstream poetry, it was the non-aligned, the external, the peripheral poets who produced poetry that was stylistically innovative. It is these authors who future students of Italian poetry will need to explore.

Tellus is the Roman goddess of the fertility of the soil, but also the goddess of the dead and the protector from earthquakes. Her cult was probably the official Roman religion's oldest one, seeming to hark back to a similar cult of the Great Mother practiced before the rise of an agricultural and pastoral society. The cult of Tellus was celebrated on April 15, with the festival of Forcididia. Over time, however, the goddess increasingly came to be associated with Ceres, and the two festivities merged into one. Tellus, along with Ceres, is cited by Ovid as one of the "harvest mothers" (*frugum matres*). This is the complex background to the myth associated with the goddess of female fertility and fertility of the soil. The title of de Palchi's work, *Foemina Tellus* (2010), references this framework and captures in this one single word, *tellus*, the heart of his oeuvre, the central motor and the source of inspiration for his poetry. On one side is the passive female image, hidden inside the inmost recess of darkness, awaiting fertilization from the numinous, virile god, the male god of fertility, who, however, metes out death and bloodshed, slaughter and negativity. The female and the male form the bedrock of de Palchi's imagery, his use of poetic language, his choice of words, and his bruising pictures. This explains the tirelessly percussive quality of de Palchi's vocabulary, where masculine words are replaced by feminine ones (*passeri* into *passere*) and, the other way round, how he turns feminine into masculine words: "On December the tenth / death was born / a companion / a spouse stretching her thighs to welcome / my life into the sulfur."

Another feature of his poetry is how objective and discursive language is replaced by an affective-effractive and emotive one. We can describe this quality with the term "connotation," that is, the ability to work "abnormities" into the fabric of the poetic discourse, distorting and misshaping the narrative sequence, even inserting frequent instances of linguistic impertinence, hyperbole, expletives, words that deform, semantic shifts, psycholinguism, the language of the unconscious, the departure from the norm of linguistic conscience, the departure from tradition, unconscious and conscious word-slips. Even when de Palchi's poetic language comes out in a denotative-declarative form, he exploits this to better explode its connotative character with an apparent denotative declaration. The system of connotation makes its appearance as a hidden, or secondary, set of signifiers in relation to the denotative plane, but we are still dealing with an extremely cunning stylistic mask, an artifice. A typical example of the literary procedure is the caption opening the final section of *Foemina Tellus*:

> The voice behind this brief sequence brings the afterlife (if it exists with its hell) to reality and fearlessly breaks into pointed accusations against the town of my birth, its men who are tiny symbols of evil, and the great and small events which have shaped my story. After more than sixty years of political, legal and literary oppression and injustice, it all came pouring out of me, one poem a day, twelve texts from my legacy. With no bitterness, no evil intention, but with a constant desire for justice. (de Palchi, 2010, 80)

It is incredible how much and in what manner a psychological trauma and a traumatic fixation suffered in adolescence can last, unchanged in time, even sixty years later. In these two poems, we clearly glimpse this unconscious process, which remains as if frozen and immobilized deep down in the "underground." The characters come out very much alive and sharply contoured, as though real, and yet, they hark back to sixty years earlier; in the unconscious regions, human figures are timeless; in the poet's mind, they move immersed in an eternal present time, wandering amid his obsessions and memories in sinister flashbacks to the outrage he was a victim to. The "priest Bepo," the "priests," the "cart-drivers," even the places are as frozen in a super-historical timelessness: the "Adige River," "with seasonal rain on the roof tiles," "Porto Legnago," with its "sad Sundays." This is the origin of the peculiar, melancholy Sunday landscapes depicted by de Palchi, as for example, in this poem featuring Porto Legnago, the town where the poet was born and spent his childhood and boyhood, with his typical structuring of the verse that makes it more irregular than free, organized more in keeping with the rhythmical and symbolic needs of the unconscious than with the rules of prosody. *"Ce monde n'est qu'abusion,"* is the quotation from Villon, which introduces the volume *The Scorpion's Dark Dance* and clearly warns the reader that the speaker is not going to waste time, nor hide behind an author's usual tricks. "The key to de Palchi's poetry appears to be cannibalism," writes Sandro Montalto in his introduction to the volume. No objections here, to be sure: cannibalism as a cruel game between the victim and the torturer which, in the geography of the unconscious, is repeated and renewed in motionless time; thus, poetry that develops like a trialogue between the unconscious, the preconscious, and consciousness, and then is flung at the corrupt and obtuse world: the cry of rebellion and the symbolic revenge:

> Sad Sundays in Porto di Legnago
> for licking ice cream

or committing suicide
with everything closed
meanwhile a pair of winged lions
embedded in the wall that leads up to the bridge
over the adige majestic or devious after floods
with seasonal rain on the roof tiles
of "Via dietro mura" which from behind the church
and the perimeter wall of memory
approaches the streams
the deathly trampling of hooves and goats
no music from that place
just the deaf thud of tolling for the dead.

*

I adjust the aim of my stones against the windows
against the disoriented heads of cart drivers
and priests who wield the power
of cruelty
the horror of existence
in haystacks and hovels,

your blessing from the earthen doorway
Giuseppe Girelli priest boorish Bepo
is so defiled
that I'm handing you over to your own inquisition
using pulpit insults
ropes round your neck and a vise on your testicles
ripping open your guts at your last scream
which I want to hear
in this neverending silence
as I aim my stone

there you are, mouth cracked open amidst a pile of bones
passing judgment on women to whom you never
stopped preaching your christian poison—
may the embers that encase your slime
atone with terrifying screams
at each strike of my stone which brings justice

hurl yourself into the abyss
so your skull may split below on the rocks
of the Bussé and the canal
forever be your hell.
(*Paradigm 2013*, 505–507)

Chapter Eleven

Alfredo de Palchi's Poetry in the New Millennium

Apropos of Nihil, The Aesthetics of Equilibrium, *and* Eventi terminali

Some time ago, a Milanese review asked me to write a psychoanalytical essay on Alfredo de Palchi's debut poetry collection, *The Scorpion's Dark Dance*, which the poet wrote between 1947 and 1951, as a twenty-year-old convict in the penitentiaries of Procida and Civitavecchia. I set about this task with a reverential curiosity and discovered in the poems a way with words, images, totems, splinters, and relics from the mind of a very young prisoner trying desperately to survive, fragments of a dialogue with his unconscious, a storm of unresolved conflicts that no psychoanalysis can (happily enough!) ever set right; excerpts from his testament on his relationship with his mother, and a father who—I did not know this at the time—had left the family long before. Non-communicating vessels of fragments that speak and communicate to one another, albeit in different and incommunicable languages. This is the poet's unconscious that pours into a book of poems. It all became clear to me in a flash. I must give my thanks to that Milanese review, and to its editor, Donatella Bisutti, who gave me the assignment. I sent my essay to de Palchi; he read it and immediately commented: "You have totally revealed me! Nobody has ever dug so deep into my unconscious!"

I believe that a critic of contemporary poetry is a sort of police chief who investigates the scene of the crime, picks up the subtle clues that hide behind the facts and the words, in an effort to correctly interpret the words and the facts as gleaned from the secondary scene. A text is a sort of "secondary scene" of the crime; the hermeneutical scholar needs to comb the place with a flashlight, seeking the scattered fragments that not even the poet knows he has used in his poems. He needs to do what amounts to a police investigation, seeking in the "primary scene" the hidden or subtly dissimulated words and symbols, of which the poetic text is a symbolic transposition on the imaginary plane.

Joseph Brodsky wrote: "You can understand a lot of things about an author by the way he places an adjective." But the opposite is equally true. Let me paraphrase: "You can understand a lot of things about an author by the way he places a noun." De Palchi has his own way of closing in on both adjectives and nouns, be it at the end of the line, in expulsion, in exile, or in the middle of a line, in a state of grammatical constriction, immediately followed by the grammatical object. There is no doubt at all that de Palchi's poetry is pre-syntactic, and it is so because it is pre-grammatical. The poet experiences a constant need to cauterize the texture of meaning of the poetic discourse with burns and ulcerations. His object is to lay a never-ending trap for the words that have lost their status of meaning. This is why his poetry is pre-experimental—nay, pre-historical. And this is why it is pre- and post-experimental as well, for he sidesteps the historical crossroads that most of Italian twentieth-century poetry bowed to without demur. But his work is also alien to the topical quality we find in so much European poetry today. De Palchi has an irresistible urge to wriggle out of mainstream poetic discourse and to remove the discourse from the recognizable places. And here, perhaps, we catch a hint of the poet's self-imposed exile at a young age. In him there is never a place: If anything, there are swift and angered glimpses onto a vista of mnemonic rubble. He is not a rational poet: He wants to catch hold, tear away Maya's veil, break Pandora's box.

This is why his poetry lurches forward, zigzagging, leaping and stumbling, ripping, in psychic frames that unravel and deflect, often skipping the copula, cutting from omission to unintentionality.

THE SLIPKNOT OF CONSCIENCE: *NIHIL*

With *Sessions with My Analyst*, de Palchi became the first twentieth-century Italian poet to use the verse fragment as a basic building block for his poetic work. The book collects the poems he wrote as a young man while serving time in the penitentiaries of Procida and Civitavecchia, after being convicted for murder on trumped-up charges and sentenced to life imprisonment. Those years of existential agony and feverish creativity led him to fashion the first Italian poetry in fragment form. *Sessions with My Analyst* came out with Mondadori in 1967, minus the poet's first collection, *The Scorpion's Dark Dance*, which the author himself decided to leave out and published in the United States in 1993.

The first edition of *Paradigma* was released in Italy in 2001, with a selection of de Palchi's poetry through 2001, while a second, augmented *Paradigma* appeared in 2006; then the even larger, bilingual *Paradigm* was issued in the United States in 2013, with not only selected and new poems (1947–2009) but also many samples from *Foemina Tellus* that were not included in the Italian edition. The title implies an awareness on the part of the author of the gulf separating his work from Italian mainstream poetry in those same years. "Paradigm shift" is an expression currently used to signify a revolutionary change in a prevailing worldview. The expression was coined by Thomas S. Kuhn in his weighty opus, *The Structure of Scientific Revolutions* (1962), to describe a change in the fundamental assumptions underpinning a dominant scientific theory. In the history of literature, new paradigms don't just rain down from the sky. When the new seeks to make its mark, it must leave the old paradigm behind in order to seek fresh legitimacy vis-à-vis the traditional worldview. By looking at the object in a new way we attain a new world vision. The most important changes of this kind occurred in the 1950s and 1960s. In this connection, de Palchi's book *Sessions with My Analyst* is key and well ahead of its time. This fact was not grasped by his contemporaries in Italy. Similarly, his volume *Paradigm* signals and highlights the uniqueness and exemplarity of his oeuvre in the panorama of Italian poetry in the second half of the twentieth century.

> Nothing certain
> rises from the spiritual archaic seas—
> my arms gesture to the skies foundering
> off-balance in the green caves of valleys
>
> conscious mutation
> vesicle pulled inside out, metamorphoses,
> through chasms of algae and fish,
> not that I'm different—being
> the excrescence working in this same
> epoch
>   and everywhere the maws of fishes
>   sharpen on others
>
> the sea an immense crater—
> and fish graffiti fixed on distance
> don't dart where now the uprooted
> gull is the only dimension aware of
>   that still unattainable flash.
> (*Anonymous Constellation*, 13)

In *Nihil*, de Palchi returns to the mythical river that symbolizes his "childhood and boyhood": the "Adige," "only the Adige remains inside me." The river represents both the return of the repressed content and the slipknot of conscience, a contradiction that can never be healed and that spawns this mnemonic diary of a time going far back into the past and coming back to the mind like a blunt weapon. The *prosimetrum* or, rather, the rhythmical prose it is written in has its root in the hurt he has carried with him ever since his youthful years; hence the lacerated, accident-prone, even, I should say, violated fabric of the language, which has lost its epicenter or, better yet, is now a place of many epicenters. In short, in these new poems of de Palchi's, we sense a subterranean quaking in the use of syntax and words, as though language eluded him, breaking away from his tools and rendering the expression here struck, adulterated, incapacitated. But, paradoxically, this is precisely the book's greatest asset: It is a vehicle of the crisis Italian poetry is currently undergoing. Yury Tynianov had already written, in the 1920s, that "poetry can exist also without prosody," and de Palchi seems to have taken this dictum literally by constructing a prose style based on the rhythms of vertical dissonances:

1
with the church bell jarred out of tune from electrical fractures, I'm the tower with the telescopic eye inside the world

2
along hedges at night, picking up snails, my hand bloodstained from brambles frescoes my face mangled by the jagged mouth swallowing up the abyss from the universe; and over these snail paths you explore the continent sunken into the abyss, no evil pertains to my little net

3
effort of life amid perversity to give up, for an orbit of equality, wading across the almost dried-up river and then to shout in dystonia for help

4
for you with your Egyptian obelisk's linear figure I'm the regret the outlaw of the outskirts of the species; fit me out with your metal in ancient underground passages; if you're the special stone among the heaped-up stones of the Assyrians the housefly of the name bleeds out from the iron of the crown; or it flies in the face rainbowing sandstorms and drought through the water of your extension

5
I'll never tear off the wings propelling you to the top or to the very bottom where you'd find the certainty of honey; you're like a child sucking the juice from squeezed orange slices off your fingers while in the chest the bellows are growing hot; blowing, scorching the universally poor face, breaking eardrums and the exegesis of cretaceous ankles, of obelisks around the now fake face of Nefertite clinging to the legs of the Sphinx

6
decades before science I foresaw 120 years of biological anguish discussing
poetry with me who imagine a long life for it invoke it with therapeutic harmony
against death helping me along to the death-rattle through the powder keg

7
in the afternoon I draw fiery off-key lines in the nothingness . . . I don't write
them down from memory, they'd give a different indication of the original
opening line: "I write with a pornographic mind," hymn about the duties of
exalted flesh

8
off you run to work . . . it's not me who's readying to carve the sandstone in
the sun, the oak tree with its branches embracing other branches hanging over
a rocky bed all the way to the sloping bank of the ditch; the fast downpour
lightning thunder flood are thrashing a plowed field; it's as you wish, or inside
the ruined house

(*Nihil* 2017, 71–85)

For over fifty years, the poetry of de Palchi has lived off the conflict
between sound and sense, sound and signifier, sound and signified. It is a
conflict that takes the shape of a phonological slippage from actant to epithet,
inasmuch as the latter goes down a semantic path of collision with the for-
mer. This fact yields a wealth of acute phonemes with a harsh, grating sound,
contrasting with a low number of other, less sharp actants. More than a syn-
esthesia between sound and sense, de Palchi uses a phonematic and semasio-
logical opposition between the words to lead them back to their full linguistic
visibility. His adverbs are always diagonal to the meaning, and this always
points to an improper modality of the modus; they serve the purpose of de-
automatizing language. In de Palchi's poetry there is not only a "discord"
between sound and sense but also a percussive intervention; the poet always
prefers an effractive, frontal solution, as if intending to rupture the language
he belongs to, in order to give a clue of his estrangement from it and of his
self-imposed exile at a young age. This is the effractive procedure de Palchi
brings into being. Thus, it is the context that changes the sound—a scratched,
clumsy sound—making it "sharp" and "flat," as Jakobson teaches us, with
lexical infection and semantic proximity. De Palchi adopts the inverse action by bending the sense to adapt it to the expression, given that words are
essentially malleable because they are a unit of seeds. It is in his use both of
verse and the poetic syntagma that de Palchi's poetry finds its raison d'être,
like a magic spell in reverse (i.e., no longer of the by-now-obsolete and un-
recoverable symbolist type, but of a post-symbolist, modernist style). It is

a rupturing spell careful with the chemistry of words, their fault lines, their electric awkwardness. De Palchi tackles the phonemic and sense context by making the seeds of language clash, triggering sparks not so much between signifiers as between meanings, rendering them unimaginably distorted and agglutinated. The result is lexemic distortions, neologisms, neo-barbarisms. We are far removed from any suggestion of a Mallarméan symbolist style, and extremely close to a typically modernist methodology that seeks phonic and phonemic expressiveness through a sense of violated and crippled seeds.

It is de Palchi himself who tells us at the beginning with this caption:

This invitation to return to the watery area where I was born and grew up until I was seventeen years old arrives more than half a century later; I accept it out of curiosity, as a wager with myself and arrogance; so let me read, modestly—to the hundred and fifty of you gathered in this room of the small local Fioroni Museum—the following intimate nostalgic variations that I have written for this occasion, illustrated by poems informing you about my naive, insolent, respectable, uncomfortable, shy, and sullen childhood and teenage years . . . (de Palchi 2017, 13)

This is all we need to understand that we are dealing with a return to the origins, to that trauma both personal and historical that invalidated his presence in this world and branded it for good, almost like an imprint on the shape of his writing and a sort of caustic information aggregated to his poetic DNA segment, which returns compulsively, even after so many years, to work underground in his choice of language.

There are tectonic-linguistic fault lines that clash and grate against other deeper and higher tectonic fault lines, linguistic-volcanic eruptions, landslides: fractures, fissions, frictions, lexical stridencies.

It is incredible how an author on the threshold of his ninetieth year still manages to be fresh and untrammeled as spring water, writes Maurizio Cucchi in his introduction to the volume. Indeed, it is incredible, but only for the reader who has not followed de Palchi down this half century of his writing. De Palchi spellbinds words like a musician does with notes, composed off the musical staff, with word-noises, distorted lexemes, implausible phrastic structures.

And so, once again, the I overwhelms the reader. The following is his self-portrait in *Nihil*:

43

the old lion, chased, hunted, wounded several times and yet unscathed, proud, brave; a tailor-made dignity that suits me. You look at his regal, proud, noble face that shows no signs of cowardliness; not the vulgar mug of a man consider-

ing himself superior enough to the "lion" and the nobilities of nature to eliminate them; this is how you'd like to eliminate the old lion that I am

53

I have neither god nor religion and rightly foresee with my verbal hate that
the planet will break loose from its centrifugal force; although I have the inner strength to do so, I refuse to prop up the planet on my back; what covers it
won't hold me down on the merry go-round while it's bursting to bits through
the abyss; my puffing on the cover of pine trees is like puffing on a "dandelion"
head from which flutter off white threads that never again will pollinate

50

you've always been here yet you don't care about dark mater, that mysterious
invisible substance weighing more than the visible universe; what effect explod-
ing supernova and neutron stars have; what you might suggest when a massive
star that has run out of its own supply of nuclear fuel begins its everlasting free
fall; a massive star that falls forever into a black hole without ever reaching the
bottom, infnite infnity; with your power to undo I assume you haven't even a
flash of mathematical intuition; you're just the corpse

54

no intention to deride you; I observe you're as curious about me as I'm about
you perched like a vulture on the back of the chair my cats use to stay near me;
instinctively they know who you are, what you're waiting for, what you're doing, whom you represent; they're thinking about it, expressing your language
from their sad muzzles, and even if you are yourself the first victim of life, being disrespectful they don't fear your vulture-like death-god look; the ancestor
gene splits, dividing the apes and evolution, while the evolving brain invents
a horrible god in its own image to abolish its own terrors and to terrorize the
other living beings of the species; death is god, the god-death, the human being
evolved into a perfect predator

33

the neighbor lady bids me to come into a plowed field during a fierce thunder
and lightning storm; at the very moment we're rolling in the mud and tits and
pubes are being drenched by the torrential rain, you startle me, repudiating the
unfaithful woman who faces up to you in the sludge of the field with . . . that
Summer of thunder and lightning and downpours of Vivaldi's Four Seasons; but
you're already planning how better to keep an eye on me next Autumn

34

I don't have enough shrewdness to compete with yours, and in this way you'll
eliminate me while I'm stubbornly competing with your skill at bewildering

even a crook; thus respect me at least out of empathy so you'll give up one last time if I confront your ultimate intention

35

pregnant? possibly you are, your assiduous big belly a world map covered with carcasses of all kinds and human carrion greedily gulped down in order to be vomited out by a brazen, belittled, regenerative mother

36

my mind gives me not a moment's peace . . . herds driven with terror into slaughterhouses; acts of opprobrium you carry out daily, the extreme fatigue of quartering, streams of blood hidden by the gleeful torture; I wish I could hug every victim, gargle with my blood the definition of their iniquitous holocaust

37

I'll be standing there gripping my head in my hands so as not to be stunned and wounded by the moaning of those doomed to the only true powerless daily holocaust; no god rules over the discomfort and evil obstinacy of human remains

38

you're the invincible one of my desires reduced to crumbs and gravel, the long narrow passages between walls clogged with the clatter of coagulated blood, the rancorous rust of the living already rotten before they burst from the womb; for this mess you're the invincible patient, butterfly, worm, oily lump, fossil

39

you take on tragic airs with me, showing yourself off like this because you possess the righteousness of ancient revengeful tragedy; it's embarrassing to have you come on stage always at the last moment with the skill of an actor who embraces all the significance from the first to the last wail; you and I haven't yet collided in that unpleasant scene

40

sixteen thousand planets similar to the earth each with a sun and satellites inhabit our part of the universe; who are the inhabitants and how do they react; you reveal nothing, managing immanence with the precision of a professional with no fixed hours; I who have them never know whether to take you seriously or scorn you to your face, universal insult
(*Nihil* 2017, 134–177)

And as he opens the section "Ombre 1998" in *Nihil*:

This invitation to return to the watery area where I was born and grew up until I was seventeen years old arrives more than half a century later; I accept it out of curiosity, as a wager with myself and arrogance; so let me read, modestly—to the hundred and fifty of you gathered in this room of the small local Fioroni Museum— the following intimate nostalgic variations that I have written for this occasion, illustrated by poems informing you about my naive, insolent, respectable, uncomfortable, shy, and sullen childhood and teenage years; . . . in the final reckoning, after more than a half-century, I have no further use for these lands, not even as a background; it's rather my homeland that needs me, and I ain't there . . . Only the Adige remains inside me . . . (*Nihil* 2017, 13)

> If I could do away with the enormous doubt
> that nags my Franciscan memory,
> but you, Adige,
> gather gravel along the contours of your shores
> and in the liquid of nets
> catch the pike that flashes brightly
> in the sandy current of the afternoon
> sunny as the doubt is dark;
> then serene once more, you reach the curves
> high with grass and shrubs, and here swirl
> hurling yourself against the pillars
> of rusty bridges that lurch
> until you toss yourself calmly toward the space
> precisely there where it doesn't exist.
> (*Nihil* 2017, 13)

Following the previous two above-cited passages, de Palchi continues as follows:

> 2
> it's my mythical river and I intend to drift down it, with anecdotes and poems, into the youthful years before my life was hunted down and driven into an exile full of vituperation invectives tortures allegations imprisonment nasty articles by anonymous gutless reporters, assertions later rendered null and void in court; the wounds and the six wasted years remain; but here, on the contrary, the torturers are still usurping even their own graves.
> (*Nihil* 2017, 17)

THE AESTHETICS OF EQUILIBRIUM

According to Theodor W. Adorno, "The fragment is the intrusion of death into the work. While destroying it, it removes the stain of semblance" (Adorno 2002, 361). Like the "trace," the "fragment" prefers to inhabit parataxis. Both are of paramount importance in the poetry of de Palchi.

These as yet unpublished fragments of aphorisms signal that once upon a time there was an earthquake, whose traces can be seen in these shavings, the traces, these scratches, these flashes. Language is reduced to pseudo-aphoristic shreds, scraps, fragments in conflict that seek no peace but rather, on the contrary, seek to be set down on paper just as they emerge from the poet's inner being. At the bottom of the constructive principle of the unstable and conflict-ridden system that is peculiar to this unpublished work of de Palchi's, we can glimpse, as through a psychoanalytical magnifying lens, a sort of transposition of a primordial text (the "thing") that has been repressed and thus disappeared.

De Palchi's creative writing possesses this feature. It wishes at all costs to appropriate the "thing," to enter inside it, to reckon with the "thing" that lies at the dark bottom of the unconscious, to make poetry "outside meaning," "outside the signifier." We must ask ourselves: What is the "thing"?

For Jacques Lacan the "thing" is not "something"; nor is it a thing that is inherently inexpressible; nor is it a noumenon. Instead, it is a result of the action of language on the real. Language acts on the real by translating it, rendering it negative, and in so doing produces by subtraction a "remainder" of its action: the "thing", the real remnant that the signifier can no longer reabsorb.

Thus, between language and the "thing," there grows a structural bond of mutual implication, which Lacan points out in his other fundamental proposition: "There is identity between the modeling of the signifier and the introduction into reality of a blissful opening, of a hole"[1] (Terzi 2013, 140), for the same event has two faces that occur simultaneously, with one as the remainder of the other. It is also in relation to language that we can posit such a notion as accessibility of the "thing." The "thing" is radically exterior to language because in itself it is neither expressible nor representable; it is "outside meaning" but also intimate with language in that it is a result of language; and, once this has happened, the void of the "thing" lodges inside the chain of signifiers and stops it from being total.

For Lacan, the "thing" is radically "outside meaning" and so basically "shrouded," alien and irreducible to any meaning we may try to express it with; the fact that this level lodges beyond meaning corrodes the subject itself in the act of experiencing; the "thing" is already "lost forever." Having once entered language, the object of the first mythical enjoyment is "already lost forever"; the experience begins with the loss and erasure of the source, and if the object of pleasure is by its nature a recovered object, the fact that "it has been lost is the consequence—after the event, however—of its having been recovered, without it being possible for us to know that it has been lost besides through these rediscoveries."

In that it is "outside meaning" and thus "lost" forever, the "thing" is never portrayed such as it is but always as a substitute for the other "thing": this is why it will always be depicted as a void, because it cannot be portrayed by anything else; or, more exactly, because it cannot but be represented by something else.

As we have seen, the "thing" in de Palchi is the negative trace, the trace of a void, an area of darkness of all that was fixed libidinally and emotively during his incarceration; it is a constellation of meanings that refuse to be placed in a logical and causal order, that reject any rationalization or secondary reconstruction of the events. In a certain measure, Lacan's theorization can help us to understand the source of de Palchi's writing and the character of his highly distinctive expressivity, his semantic instability and iconological rigidity.

As we know, Lacan uses Martin Heidegger to move in his own deeply different direction. In Heidegger, this analysis fits into the framework of a phenomenological-ontological description, which tries to see events as the single thing in the encounter between mortals and the divine, earth and sky, thus somehow still within the bounds of an understanding that seeks the meaning of man's "poetic" life in the world within a given constellation of meanings. Instead, Lacan uses the void to insert inside the core of the experience a relationship that cannot be boiled down to drive and pleasure but constitutes a relationship with something that is radically "outside meaning" as well as, conceivably, "outside the signifier."

As early as *Seminar VII*, and later when Lacan developed the concept of the "object a," this void of the "thing" becomes a causative void of desire, while the "thing" is the extraneous term around which the whole movement of *Vorstellung* is seen to turn. This means that the "thing" is not simply the object of desire but the object that causes desire, the void behind which the subject causes desire and sets it into motion. The subject's experience gravitates around this elusive void that impels it. Language's "magic circle" lodges between the subject and the "pleasure" of the "thing"; the tension-torsion toward pleasure thus looks to transgress a barrier; and *Seminar VII*, as Jacques-Alain Miller notes, is the paradigm of "impossible pleasure" (Miller 1988). The void sets in motion the subject's desire for the "thing" as a full-fledged, undiminished object of pleasure, but attaining it would mean the destruction of the subject's experience, as this sustains itself precisely by its distance from both poles. The distance between the subject and *das Ding* is precisely the condition of the word.

To affirm that there is no metalanguage thus means that all utterance goes astray (and the signifiers as well) once it is placed in front of its assumptions; or, then, that the "thing" of language, the ultimate word, can only posit itself as lacking; thus, there is no language of the "thing"; therefore, Orpheus never has the vision of Eurydice as an object (cause) of desire, in that it is precisely the latter that in existence opens that void inside which the word comes into play as presence-absence, constituting something like language in the process. From this angle, the "thing" appears as a sort of exteriority inside language, an object that is impossible because it is unutterable but which, at the same time, marks in the word the economy of any manner of utterance.

It is the very conception of the subject that changes significantly with respect to the psychoanalytical tradition and Heidegger's being-in-the-world. The event of this "outside meaning," which is the "thing," corrodes the subject and etches its flesh because it conditions its entire experience. The subject pays the entrance ticket to the symbolic order by foregoing pleasure and by founding a subject that is radically eccentric in that it desires. The "beyond meaning" acts just as the subject in itself takes shape. The subject takes shape by splitting up between the linguistic-signifier domain and that remainder, "outside meaning," which is the "thing." The experience consists of the back-and-forth swing within this relationship, which is what marks its rhythm and rewrites its drama. In a certain sense, the subject itself is the "thing"; it is no longer the "in-the-world" of being, but it exists with both the "thing" and its void.

This organic bond between the subject and the "thing" also brings with it the importance of themes such as the "supplementary" and the "remainder" for a proper rethinking of the subject's statute. If the subject occurs in that differential movement between language and the real, if the "thing" is already lost and represented by something else, the experience takes shape from the point beyond which the source is cancelled and consists of a series of recoveries of replacement objects which take the place of the source that never took place as such. The subject's experience thus takes place in what Jacques Derrida describes as follows: "the strange structure of the supplement appears here: a possibility produces by delay that to which it is said to be added" (Derrida 1973, 89).

De Palchi attempts a highly seismic and chthonian writing, at the same time building a sort of anti-seismic outer structure to affect a fracture and a suture in one. This is a method of writing that proceeds and explodes out of a repression in early life, causing the break-up of a symbolic and metaphorical universe that is highly unstable and entropic. Indeed, de Palchi makes no effort to stabilize his poematic constructions; the traces and fragments are living proof thereof: Cacophonous and undisciplined, they slip towards entropy. They entropize and scatter.

The next-to-last section of *The Aesthetics of Equilibrium* is entitled "Genesis of My Death." It is a gigantomachy and ultimate peroration, the most direct and frontal soliloquy in poetic prose ever written in Italian from the twentieth century into the present century. It is an irrevocable condemnation of humankind. It starts with the hominid "anthropoid," goes through the *Homo erectus* to reach *Homo sapiens*, the most destructive and bloodthirsty animal that Mother Nature has ever begotten, given that he is equipped with consciousness, which multiplies to the nth degree his immeasurable thirst for flesh and destruction. This long poem ends with a vast explosion "from the window I an *Anthropoid* symbol of the worst evil watch the 'globe' go down at Times Square Manhattan 10 9 8 7 6 5 4 3 2 1 . . . as when a stone is tossed into the water, the bottom of the planet explodes in widening irradiating circles of massive nuclear energy."

We can conclude that de Palchi resolves Heidegger's question of authenticity in his own way. The "public realm" is now nothing but ideology; the "private realm" is now ideology: The choice between the two opposites is a false problem. Speculation regarding authenticity posited a priori is bogus and can be thrown into the bin. There will be no other principle. And there will be no other end than this one. With the end of humankind, nothing will change, and the universe will continue its mad race towards cooling and entropy. Indeed, de Palchi's is a spiritual testament irrevocably condemning humankind.

It is a poetry of the "trace" which appears as a naked presence: trace, in that it is what remains after the original imprint has been deleted. It is not by chance that all this poetry is constructed in the present tense, with frequent use of deictic words, which go well with verbs conjugated in the present tense. The poetry of the absolute trace is possible only by declining its imaginary universe in the present tense. It is the non-presence of the unconscious that is revealed in this writing's presence-absence. The poetry appears as the drift of the unconscious non-presence. Even the obsession for places harking back to the poet's youth, so plentiful in de Palchi's poetry, reveals the non-presence and the lack of the absolute place. The here and now is the indescribable place of the absolute present, of now. This theory of non-presence can be led back to the concept of the trace. The trace, which Derrida borrows from Emmanuel Lévinas, is a past that has never been never present; it is the dimension of an otherness which has never appeared and can never appear, and which Derrida does not hesitate to liken to the psychoanalytical notion of the unconscious.

We can now understand why de Palchi's poetry appears as the supplement of an absence in a web of scattered traces. Because this is its raison d'être, the way to attain a web of shifts, transmissions, postponements.

Like the Freudian notion of the unconscious, the concept of the trace in de Palchi takes on an anti-symbolist function, in the sense that it constitutes an order of otherness which, by definition, is unrepresentable or representable only through the chain of replacements, of traces of language. Derrida states that to describe or read the traces of "unconscious" traces (for there is no such thing as a "conscious" trace), the language of presence or absence as also the metaphysical discourse of phenomenology are both inadequate.

This, indeed, is the main outcome given by the concept of the trace: to convey that the order of meaning (of conscience, of presence, and of the whole conceptual system which they regulate; i.e., the entire system of metaphysics) is a supplementary order, in this manner radicalizing what, in accordance with that system of metaphysics, was a condition confined to writing pure and simple. In other words, the unrepresentable trace has a tendency to make one interpret every presentation or representation as that which stands in the place of the "first" trace; just as consciousness (which Sigmund Freud likens to a "magic notebook" in a well-known text, and which Derrida discusses in his *Writing and Difference*) is the visible trace of the unconscious. The logic of the supplement is obviously unthinkable within the system of logic, as Derrida wrote in *Of Grammatology*: The supplement makes up for a lack, a non-presence, in the sense that it represents the moment of structuring which is not preceded by anything but thanks to which something "appears" (Derrida 1997). "The supplement takes the place of a yielding, of a non-meaning or a non-represented, of a non-presence. There is no present coming before it, and thus, it is only preceded by itself; i.e., by another supplement. The supplement is always the supplement of a supplement" (Derrida 1997).

The project of a new modernist poetry in Italy is something I have time and again promoted. Opposition to anything new in this field has, over time, targeted de Palchi's work with much hostility. But mine is no less than a call for us to reclaim a poetry no longer viewed as a self-justifying discourse (i.e., a propositional discourse in the manner of experimentalism, based on the autonomy of the signifier and the heteronomy of the signified). One cannot compose poetry if one has in mind the autonomy or heteronomy of the signifier in poetic language, as Luciano Anceschi adialectically thought back in the 1950s. There is a "sense" that poetry must necessarily pursue, and this is irrespective of the signifier's autonomy, lest it expire. And poetry must pursue this sense even today, when the direction becomes daily more obscure and undecipherable.

When I think of the poems of *Sessions with My Analyst*, and, in general, the whole of de Palchi's oeuvre, I grow more and more convinced that his originality lies in that constant circling round of its mysterious object, the "thing." This is the secret power of his poetry. Even in his last two collections, *Nihil* and *The Aesthetics of Equilibrium*, we detect how de Palchi is endlessly free in the manner of his discourse, free to range at will, to leave the theme behind him and then go back to it, to contradict himself, free from any conditioning by schools, precepts, fashions, free not to follow any propositional poetic discourse, no euphonic or cacophonic model unhappily in vogue in today's neo-narrative poetry. De Palchi seeks no dissonance for dissonance's sake nor an alleged originality; he never chases after special effects but always stands firm on his ground, waiting to shoot his sharp shafts at the murderous anthropoid. There is a powerful impolitic and unpoetic charge in this icono-clastic fury of his, which also has repercussions on his syntax and the poetic "model" that underpins and sustains it. It is a way of making poetry with no safety net below. It is a new and different vision of the poetic Logos. I would call it an ontological vision of writing poetry. For all these reasons, I see de Palchi as a forerunner of a different way of understanding the discourse of poetry in the Italian context. Yes, there may well be something anarchic in it: How he addresses the matter at hand and how he sees the goal of poetic dis-course may well be impolitic, but they represent the most compelling effort made in Italian poetry in the second half of the twentieth century, and into our present century, to knock down the propositional model of poetic discourse that has been practiced in this country, and, in general, in Western countries, for the past sixty to seventy years. For me, this is sufficient to take de Palchi's poetic work as an example of great intellectual courage.

This is why I also choose to take de Palchi's poetry as an outpost (eschew-ing the word "avant-garde," now devoid of sense) for a different way of or-ganizing the poetic discourse, free of all stereotypes, formalistic prejudices, and schools.

Here follows the sequence "Genesis of My Death" from *The Aesthetics of Equilibrium*:

1

It's an over-abundant self-appraising authoritative domineering shrewd rac-ist violent animal with a unique baseness belonging to fauna that domi-nate all the other species . . . in ancient Latium the legionary anthro-poid conquers and builds civilizations in the west south east north . . . he impartially presumes that you, the end of everything, are the fearsome peren-nial female named Mors Moarte Mort Muerte Death . . .

2

as an anthropoid who is an enemy of the anthropoid I ascertain that you are the prototype of the sensitive intuitive female more than the masculine *Tod*-figure in the north . . . a massive more fearsome barbarian than you a female to the centu-rions of Germanicus . . . the massive Tod dance glows in the flames licking ash and injustice off the furnaces . . . you arrive blameless at the noxious moment within which you lower the eyelids over each existence . . .

3

November 2nd All Soul's Day standing next to their tumulus are those hostile
to the Garden of Eden that they've destroyed leaving no remembrance of the
myth . . . a day that turns into unreal weirdness when multitudes of the living
dead stroll jauntily through the cemetery . . . they're reading unknown people's
gravestones and placing chrysanthemums on the gravestone of someone they
once knew . . . a precarious ssssss whisper invades the tombs . . . from a scoundrel each dead person becomes honest but a scoundrel he remains through the
ever-living anthropoid who never ceases being a rogue and the murderer of the
meek animals from the mythological Garden of Eden . . . the day of rotten flow-
ers doesn't mislead you from reaching the equitable slaughter . . .

4

to my conception I conceive your presence and in what moment of parental
obscenities a supernal understanding starts up between us . . . for months deliri-
ous because of an evil infesting me in the arms of the young mother who can't
breastfeed me anymore . . . when I am three you bring me back to life on my tri-
cycle at the bottom of steps down which a playmate's infantile envy has pushed
me . . . you bring me back to life a second time when the same small anthropoid
forces me to grasp an electric wire . . . my body keeps shaking until the arrival
of my grandfather who hears me screaming . . . you're my protector and savior
from my unconscious to my consciousness . . . your pungent incense-like scent
removes me from the smells of the living dead who hate you without understanding what I gratefully understand about you . . . the living and the perennial
dead hate you because I welcome your benevolence . . .

5

in my mind I consciously get close to you Our Lady of Elsewhere as you make
yourself known through puffs of air gently touching me in a sign of protection
. . . you protect me from the Nazi SS in Peschiera in November 1943 when they
amusedly measure my sixteen-year-old head without suspecting a culturally
criminal significance . . . a single millimeter of difference can define me as a
Jew . . . a Jew according to the self-styled science of the Austrian phrenologist
Franz Joseph Gall.

6

autumn 1944 in Villabartolomea German troops and the black brigades return
from rounding up rebels at the ends of the lower Veronese valleys . . . my blonde
girlfriend Ginetta warns me not to take the ferry across the Adige . . . through
this girlfriend you make me avoid a barrage of bullets from the ferry that hit
two brigade soldiers on the dock . . . I never ask my twenty-year-old girlfriend
to clarify my suspicion . . . we love each other and you who protect me know
when good is sometimes stronger than evil . . .

7

27 April 1945 . . . four anthropoid thugs armed with guns and lugers position themselves a few feet in front of me . . . as a devastated adolescent anthropoid I study the four faces and am unsure whether they'll shoot me in the square next to a shop window full of fabrics . . . some American soldiers quickly arrive and put an end to the scene by slapping the four faces with a redneck bandana around their necks . . . in the district prisons they blotch up my back with a leather strap . . . while I'm lying on the wooden floor they kick me with their heavy boots burn my armpits with pages of L'Arena . . . and force me to swallow a bowl of soapy water full of beard shavings . . . you my salvation hear my cries for help and free me from their evilness one after another within two months . . . one is crushed by a truck while he is riding a motorcycle . . . two drown in the Adige . . . and Nero Cella name and legal last name is convicted of rape and armed robbery . . . and six years later you free me from that autumnal evil spell in the Seine . . .

(*Estetica dell'equilibrio* 2017)

A PSYCHO-PHILOSOPHICAL
INVESTIGATION OF *EVENTI TERMINALI*

The Uncanny (1919) is one of Freud's key works. It provided the groundwork for *Beyond the Pleasure Principle*, published in 1920. Freud sees the "uncanny" as the result of the emergence of something like a "death drive," a pull toward a primordial state, dwelling in the heart of the "pleasure principle" that the maestro of psychoanalysis was then investigating. Now, for the "uncanny."

This concept allows us to reference the theories of Heidegger and Lacan, who both speak of estrangement (*Unheimlichkeit*) as a state triggered by the encounter with an outsider or with someone who is familiar to us, with something which is our very own and has been so for a long time but which we have grown distant from; something which, as it appears in our consciousness, shakes the construction of our identity and reality. As we know, Freud was the first to speak in these terms of the "uncanny," with a linguistic analysis that underlined the polysemy of the word *heimlich* (which can even overlay its opposite, *unheimlich*), and defined it as something once repressed that comes back, something that is "familiar to mental life from very ancient times and estranged from it only because of the process of repression" (Freud 1997, 217).

According to Freud, this coming to the surface is made easier and also evoked by certain situations, such as dealing with what has some relationship with death, having doubts about being, in fact, dead, or meeting the figure of the "double," thus calling into question the I. Watching the duplication of the I in a perpetual return to itself. According to Freud, in the course of time, the I develops a sort of defense against the rest of the I. But there are unrealized possibilities the imagination is not ready to relinquish, as well as aspirations that have not been satisfied for external reasons. Both may then become part of the figure of the "double," which, though at first affording relief and pleasure, gradually grows troublesome, anguishing in its recalling "a time when the ego had not yet marked itself off sharply from the external world and from other people" (Freud 1997, 212). The same thing happens with the "omnipotence of thoughts" used by primitive man and the child; whenever it surfaces in adult life, it shakes the confines rationality has built and becomes distressing.

This is the reason for de Palchi's nomenclatural fury with respect to the "anthropoids," those "thugs" that "blotch up," "kick," "gragragragra blood pours into the bucket."

Uncanny is then the return of something we had shut out when we built our identity. Freud says that this can also be something extremely pleasant, something that in another period of our life was useful and reassuring but now has become unpleasant and dangerous because it undermines a balance built on its exclusion. What follows, as a result of the appearance of the uncanny, is, in fact, the I feeling that it has lost control, its powerlessness. Something returns, but its return was not wished for. Another example of the uncanny is the repetition of events that the subject takes on in a totally passive manner. What in itself could be harmless may, due to this demoniacal repetition, in-spire fear, and this is what Freud calls the "repetition compulsion," something the I now sees as other to it. Freud goes so far as to affirm that the uncanny is "all that which can recall this deep repetition compulsion" (Freud 1997, 215). The distress is generated not so much by what inspires fear but by its some-how getting back into contact with a sort of primal magma, which threatens to swallow us up yet which is also the basis for any project or desire of ours. The emergence of something frightening is "nothingness," this repetition compul-sion or, as Lacan would have it, the total pleasure, the "double," the "other," the "outsider," the "familiar," the "twin," de Palchi's "Eugenio."

This is de Palchi: "Which of us two pretends to be the poet?"

The nightmare that becomes an obsession. The familiar that becomes strange, with a sense of vertigo and an oversized I as its outcome; the feel-ing of "emptiness" and the dizzy plunge towards that "emptiness" which the author also discovers to be "full"; the fear that becomes pleasure, the pleasure of mastering again the ideational content deriving from the repetition compulsion, which, in turn, leads him to curse the "totems," "doubles," "triple hoodwinkers," and "anthropoids" which recur and return to crowd the poet's mind. Thus the anguish, and the pleasure of this anguish for having enabled him to meet the challenge of a resurfacing of the repressed content, the "twin," that "Eugenio" (Eugenio Montale), the author of *Cuttlefish Bones* ("which attracts rogues, poetasters, bootlickers"), which is the most polished and refined work of twentieth-century Italian poetry in contrast to his own, which is "harsh, essential."

De Palchi proclaims: "no anthropoid is innocent of his own ugliness"; "nobody is innocent." Here we sense his satisfaction at having castigated humankind, reduced to such "ugliness," to a motley group of crooks, and at the same time, the pleasant dizzy feeling that accompanies these curses. Thus, the mechanism of anguish gets going again every time the stability of the I is in jeopardy due to the return of the repetition compulsion, together with a renewal of the nomenclatural "omnipotence."

Freud often asks himself why people continue, at times for their whole lives, to repeat unpleasant incidents. He hypothesized that the repetition is an attempt to get the upper hand, to tie down once and for all the excitement they generated and so find solace again.

Freud assumes that pleasure and its opposite depend on the amount of "free excitement," and for the principle of pleasure to act, excitement must be "discharged" so that quiet can return. Our consciousness does the job of tying down the excess of excitement. The subject is dragged backward by what Freud calls the "repetition compulsion," accompanied by the amount of anguish determined by this return. Only when free excitement is tied down successfully in this process, by means of literary elaboration and depiction, can the principle of pleasure come into play.

The latter, together with the repetition compulsion, are then not in opposition to each other but converge towards the same goal, to the neutralization of all tensions, to the discharging of excitement. We can even state that what Freud called the "death wish" works unconsciously for the principle of pleasure and so to consolidate the I.

Now we can appreciate how much de Palchi's identity is linked to a loss, a harrowing separation that coincides with the emergence of the signifier. It is, in fact, the words of poetry that try to compensate for the hole of "absence," without ever entirely succeeding. Our poet gives himself over to the words of poetry as an additional substitute for the primary laceration, through the secondary activity of writing poetry, seeking a primordial pacification, a return to the origins that can never occur.

APROPOS OF *EVENTI TERMINALI*

Maurizio Ferraris writes: "Dear Alfredo de Palchi, sooner or later, as the saying goes, the truth comes out. This is a fact. The truth (and the reality it refers to) emerges as if self-impelled, and is not constructed with men's weak faculties, as so many philosophers have immodestly insisted"[2] (Ferraris 2016, 127).

Sooner or later, the true issues of poetics and aesthetics will surface, and then we will avow that what the votaries of the literary vulgate told us was bogus and that the history of poetry in the first and second halves of the twentieth century will have to be rewritten. Much water will flow beneath the bridges, and so much poetry will pass without leaving a trace. What will endure will be a mere sprinkling, and your poetry will be there, and the weak human faculties will be powerless to hide the true state of things as they have done up to now, and your innovative poetry will stand out amidst so much other work that the passage of time will delete.

We are surrounded by "chat" words: radio, TV, the Internet, newspapers, entertainment and niche magazines, imitation poetry made of plastic; billions of words are swarming and buzzing about with a disturbing and compulsive effect on our minds. Literary works, too, are broadcast using chat words. Alas, we have no choice but to believe firmly in utopia: that only high literature can pierce through the rarefied atmosphere made of swarms of vapid, useless, and downright pernicious words. Words are important to keep the aesthetic conscience of a national community alive and vigilant. The decadence of a people's words is the sign of the progressive breakdown of a country and a language. A language reflects a precise conception of the world and is the image of the community's identity, bonded together by a common language. By changing the words, the language also changes, and so the worldview that language expresses; and thus also the mirror that community's identity is reflected in. The I's sense of identity is a linguistic construction and, as Lacan stated, what the subject understands as a signifier does not coincide with what, for the same subject, is a meaning. A gaping void opens between signifier and meaning. When a nation's identity is in crisis, the language of its best poets also grows obscure. In his latest work, *Eventi terminali*, de Palchi senses, as if by telepathy, the vast crisis that his country Italy is going through, and he translates it into a poetic work which, however ungrammatical and tattered, has enormous vigor. De Palchi's writing seeks to pierce through present-day, mainstream poetic language and does so in its own way, with a fracturing power that leaves the reader speechless. It is the language of a testament we see here: de Palchi goes back compulsively to the shattered and violated places and the events that shaped the years of his youth; he takes

Italy's greatest twentieth-century Ligurian poet, Eugenio Montale, to task and mocks him by contrasting his cloying literary style with his own unthinking and instinctive style. This is poet Alfredo de Palchi's last will.

In teleological terms, the ideal critic is the ideal reader. To grasp the "experience" that a poet's words offer us is the duty of the ideal reader, and thus the critic's as well. The critic's aim is to declare the literary worth of a text. At times, the first encounter with a text is not enough. Frequently, a careful reader will go back to a work and mull it over. He will read and reread it, even after many years. Reflection is the first stage of the process of comprehension, but inevitably, a valuation is implicit in every act of reading. The ideal reader will need to ask himself: To whom is this work addressed? Where does the work come from? In what relation does it stand vis-à-vis other works of its time? How does it relate to the works of the past? How does it stand in its own times? A critical assessment always implies classifying not only the work but also the ideal reader. However, a critical judgment is always "open"; it cannot be "closed," lest it be theological dogma. A judgment seeks to meet other judgments on a level playing field. So, the ideal reader ideally seeks to meet with other readers, to prompt him to re-examine his previous assessment. Paradoxically, the critic needs to relate to the public more than a poet or author. Without this, a critical reading would merely be a subjective response. I believe that in the framework of a community there should be an elite of intelligent readers seeking some sort of consensus on aesthetic judgments. Without the support of an intelligent readership, the work of the ideal reader becomes utopian, and the same thing goes for the critic. Finally, a critic's writings are also a testament, exactly like the poet's.

When a society does not have a literature in good health, literary criticism is diminished and rendered opaque, while the community sleeps its ontological sleep. Democracy itself is in peril. The assessment of the community's *res publica* is not so different and distinct from the assessment of such a "private thing" as a book of poems.

The defense of a book of poems has to do with a defense of democracy. To take interest in a work of poetry, to defend a good book of poems, or an author, is then a highly "political" exercise, an act that the citizen performs in the framework of the polis, an act that has to do with individual and collective freedom. Finally, we are speaking here of a public act.

NOTES

1. This passage translated by Steven Grieco-Rathgeb.
2. This passage translated by Steven Grieco-Rathgeb.

Roberto Bertoldo
Interviews Alfredo de Palchi

Roberto Bertoldo: You have lived in Italy, France, and the United States. How did each of these countries influence your poetry from both the cultural and social points of view?

Alfredo de Palchi: Preamble: In the Procida penitentiary, among the twenty or so political prisoners I shared a common dormitory with, I had the great good fortune of meeting a thirty-two-year-old army officer, Ennio Contini. I was then barely eighteen. Mind you, I speak of many things also in Ennio's name because Italy has not only for dozens of years undemocratically maintained in power the same embarrassing and shameless right- and left-wing mugs, corrupt criminals, crooks, thieves, but the country has also divided the literary scene into two blocs: one, the elect—the big publishing houses; the other, the herd—the small publishers. To be counted among the elect, it's not clear what you need to have: talent? Not always. To be counted among the herd, there is no need to go into detail. The situation gets mixed up, but you sense the air blowing you either towards the elect or towards the herd. The bloc of the elect are invested with powers to rule over the herd which, quietly bleating, accept their function of being scapegoats, or even worse, of underlings. This invisible hedge brings together the peaceable herd in its grazing grounds, refuses to stir the bottom of tainted waters. Or then a sheep here and there will dare to bleat sycophantically in the direction of the one in order of fame, laboring under the delusion that it too is an elect. But if a sheep timidly rebels, it bleats quietly to its neighbor: For god's sake, let's not make a noise.

Straddling the hedge is the dissident, the outcast, who sells himself neither to the elect nor to the herd, who gives neither the satisfaction of butchering him: This is the ideal phantasmagorical Don Quixote provocateur who whispers no flattery, who speaks out loud.

So now I come to your question, and this is my answer: the communist executioners in and around where I was born, mythomaniacs of a non-existent resistance up till the allied troops appeared, never fired a shot against the retreating German soldiers who were blowing up Verona's historic bridges.

The war over, the commanding colonels, the named and the nameless, such as the Luigi Longos and the Sandro Pertinis, acted like common criminals. All these falsehoods are still making the rounds among the apologists of the resistance movement and in the press. But they displayed great heroism in traumatizing my skinny body with the tortures I carried with me for a couple of years, shooting at my legs—a bunch of Americans in the town saved me from being killed and the officer, or corporal, whatever he was, gave my chief torturer, Nerone Cella, who saluted him with clenched fist, a tremendous punch in the nose—and by requesting the court to sentence me to death in accordance with the laws of occupation of May 1945.

I reacted to that request with a nervous smile of disbelief and terror. A bloodcurdling cry went up in the courtroom: "Wicked, wicked." In the newspaper the following day, too, came the words "with evil cynicism..." They mistook my nervous smile for a challenge. The judge, reprimanding me when I took off my jacket and shirt in the courtroom so that he could see the condition of my body, without a witness for or against me and without any proof regarding my alleged activities during the Italian Social Republic, sentenced me to life imprisonment. But of the torturers, two drowned in the Adige, one was run over by a motorbike, and my "favorite," Nerone Cella, was thrown into jail for carnal violence and armed robbery. This petty crook and criminal started having visions of Christ and [the] Virgin Mary and, with the help of the church, was freed many years before me so that he could go back to his career as a thief and a criminal before his miserable life came to an end. This is the story of the so-called resistance. I do admit that there were, and still are, communists who are gentlemen; some I got to know and befriended; nevertheless, I record the general brutality and cowardice with the contempt of the verses I wrote in 1947:

> You condemn me
> you crack my bones but can't
> touch what I think of you:
> jealous of my meaning of a neutral
> courage . . .
> (*The Scorpion's Dark Dance*, 61)

And those from 2005, which close the volume *Paradigm*:

> I who amazed find myself giving in
> to this shabby existence do not crumble

as does the ancient hovel you inhabit
you unhappy amoebae

turning plebeian to propagate the cowardly
myth of you cowardly even in your looks.
(*Paradigm* 2013, 372)

And leftist Italy continues to call whoever does not follow its ideology a "fascist," forgetting how it itself has been preaching for over sixty years. Fascism preached its ideology for only twenty years. When I was released from prison in 1951, I already considered politics a calamity. And while I was in Italy, or in Paris where I mixed with circles in Saint Germain des Prés and Montparnasse, or in Franco's Spain, where I had met people in the underground anarchist circles of Barcelona, I had a couple of mishaps. A few years later, I came to a standstill in New York City. I followed a mental anarchy free of constrictions. I considered myself apolitical: monarchist, fascist, republican, communist, liberal, socialist = anarchist, without ever wishing to blow up places or people.

Those countries undoubtedly had an influence—I don't know in what manner or how much—on my intelligence and, *en passant*, on my poetry. Zero influence on my politics. The truth is that I, not an adherent of the ballot, have rather deleterious opinions: Politicians of all types and mistypes, whether they make believe they're representing the plebe, or have been completely corrupted by the corporations, are all cowards and thieves. I have an immeasurably cynical opinion of them. Culturally speaking, a disciplined anarchist, only sociable with those of my choosing, *j'ai lu tous les livres*, at least all those I was able to read, and something must have gotten through my wild elegance. Thus I can confirm that, for the last fifty-five years, my cultural experience has been an international one.

Roberto Bertoldo: Your poetry, which often is both passionate and sarcastic, takes on love, sex, religion, lack of freedom, etc. Which of these themes do you feel closest to you?

Alfredo de Palchi: Love = sex, it would seem. A gay Swiss friend, whom I studied at the Académie Julian with, in 1952, suddenly, without any previous rhyme or reason, asked me at Argenteuil, right at my mother's place where we used to go every Sunday to have a full meal to counteract our weekly diet of bananas and beer, if I were more interested in sex or spirituality. It was normal for him to be curious, given that in the evenings he moved in his milieu, I in mine. I dumbfounded him with a sudden answer: sex. Which, however, for me, needs to have a bond with love. If love means spirituality, too, then I'm also spiritual. Yet for all that, my brain only felt, saw, and desired sex, but as a lover. The impression I had of myself was of the hungry one. I was hungry in jail, and when I went free, although I had banquets of it, I was constantly possessed—never enough of it—even though I was exhausted. My prison term had the merit of psychologically condemning me, a mere eighteen-year-old, to a sexual appetite interwoven with myths and religious icons, especially the cross, symbol of torture of a young man overflowing with love. As for me, once the comparison has been abolished, I am and remain the symbol of the tortured adolescent.

Am I a romantic? I am, privately, but not in my art. This is my physical, psychological, and mental torture: the theme love = sex, which floods my poetry. Certain erotic compositions, never vulgar, seem blasphemous to some who read them. But, if read carefully, one can sense the symbolism of my spirituality: love = sex of power and liberation.

"The lack of freedom" theme in my work must be there at the beginning, in the first collection, *The Scorpion's Dark Dance*, which I set down in the penitentiaries of Procida and Civitavecchia between 1947 and 1951 and which, organized years later, I included in the Mondadori volume of *Sessions with My Analyst*, only to take it out at the last moment before it went to press. I found it different in terms of material and style. Anyhow, for the last fifty-five years, I have known I would feel free under any dictatorship. The Stalinist one, for example, which I wished and still wish on the Italian communists ideological fanatics, such as the late intellectual Franco Fortini and that wishy-washy guy, Fausto Bertinotti. I would personally give to people like them a shovel and pick, or a hammer and sickle, so that they can earn an honest livelihood. After sixty-five years of pseudo-democracy, you feel obliged to make an ideological choice, meaning the communist one. In fact, it continues to brainwash the minds of workers and students who are dupes of labor union people and worthless teachers, and it has the audacity to accuse those who aren't communists, of being fascists! Like saying communism is "freedom."

Roberto Bertoldo: Which one of your books do you think is the most politically and socially engagé?

Alfredo de Palchi: Socially? It seems to be the Mondadori book, *Sessions with My Analyst*, as Vittorio Sereni agreed when he had it published, but which remained more or less misunderstood—new, different from the usual bullshit—by the very few reviewers who did not know how to deal with it and mauled it. I repeat, it seems socially—never politically—engagé, as the American translator I. L. Salomon suggested in his introduction in 1970. The social commitment, if there is any, is involuntary, and I'm sorry it's there.

Roberto Bertoldo: The lyricism of your writing is complex, but as regards its subjectivity, I feel that your "I," unlike other "civil" poets, only rarely can be construed as "We." Would you agree?

Alfredo de Palchi: My "I" as much as the "you," in fact, means "I" and "you." Yet "you" means "she," which means woman = sex = spirituality = earth = nature, all in the feminine gender. Never "we." If there is a "we" in my work, it is a curse, or then the text obliged me to use it. However, that "we" also means "I" and "you," my "I" and "you" imply "my" earthbound physiognomy and "hers," which both imply the universal feminine meaning of "we" = "I" and "you."

Roberto Bertoldo: But precisely this "woman," who is also "earth," "nature," is a sort of synecdoche that makes your poetry "civil" in the "universal" sense. When this happens, you are, however indirectly, a civil poet, considering how much indignation—both heretical and ironic—pervades your verses.

Alfredo de Palchi: If you interpret me as "civil" because I see "woman" as "earth" and "nature," that is, my sentiment and my vision as "universal," then I agree. You see, when a short time ago I thought myself accused of being a civil poet, I immediately saw the variations: *civil* rights, *civil* war, *civil* death, *civil* status, *etc.* Unfortunately, I experienced those injustices. That's why I was saying that I'm not a "civil" poet. We say this man is civil, this other one is not civil. "We" people believe ourselves to be chosen by the creator to be "civilized," invented long before our ape forefathers came along; with their mental obscurities caused by their constantly having to get out of danger's way, they arrive in modern times; and here "we," brutish and evil-doing people, not only consider ourselves to be civilized but feel empowered to rob and make nature progress. Frankly speaking, ever since the first glimmerings of a young "bastard" who had distanced himself away from the elect and from that progress, I have intuitively seen myself in the fertile creative femininity of woman = earth = nature.

Roberto Bertoldo: How do you see yourself in relation to symbolism, then? And the avant-garde art movements?

Alfredo de Palchi: It's my taste that rejects the poetry of the Italian nineteenth century and of the Crepuscolari, not my study of it. This is why I turned, when still a prisoner, to French poetry, assisted in this by my friend Ennio Contini. I can't say in what relation I stand vis-à-vis to symbolism. I certainly love some symbolists more than others, and if there is a relation in this sense, it means I was smarter than I thought. In fact, years later, in Paris, in 1952, I discovered a book, Marcel Raymond's *De Baudelaire au surréalisme* (it's still with me today, old and tattered and coming apart), which opened up universes in my primitivistic and anarchic ignoramus' head; had I stayed on in Italy, I would never have come across them. Show me the work of one nineteenth-century Italian "poet" who is in any way related to French symbolism. For me, that Italian period, up to the very early twentieth century, makes its appearance with weeping willows and trumpets. Still today, the trumpets, windbags, and trombones go on, and I don't think they want to know their names to avoid bumping into each other on my list. I appreciate cubist, dadaist, and surrealist poetry. At the international poetry festival in Castelfranco Veneto in 1961, I met Tristan Tzara and, being apparently the only one who wanted to get to know him, we talked for almost three days. The Neo-Avant-Garde poets and the rest of them were chasing Romanian poetesses and poets, free to be Scotch-taped to their communist commissars. If there is a relation to my work, it is because those historical avant-garde movements grew out of mouths that are still interesting. I totally reject the rancid Italian Neo-Avant-Garde movements of the 1960s. That's ballast, and I say it without regrets. There's enough inanity to make even circus clowns laugh. All those feeble and immediately outdated shots they fired in the direction of zero, and all those more or less recent arid shots they fire at each other, they don't admit that the avant-garde-ness could pop up in formal poetry with all its rhyming schemes. What I mean to say is that avant-garde, or originality, is in the text, not in the way you spread the vocabulary across the page amid commas, quotation marks, brackets, etc.

Roberto Bertoldo: For quite some time now, the academic poets have rallied in one body to destroy poetry and marginalize "expressive" poets. You, as a victim, know something about it. And so, what dangers do these academic versifiers, these traffickers of verbal death, pose both for poetry and for people?

Alfredo de Palchi: Mediocrity always exists, consecrated by every generation and every season. Partly, it's down to the prevailing taste of those called on to rule over the graveyards of poetry, at times to even willingly humiliate those who write in an individual canon. Dino Campana is an example of one cast out by your run-of-the-mill critics. Except for the rare ones, like Enrico Falqui, who identified him almost immediately—or then right after his death in an insane asylum—the rest of the critics and experts allowed him to remain unknown right up to the 1960s. Oh, yes, he's mad. In 1961, I mentioned this to Vittorio Sereni who, as an honest and upright man, admitted he had allowed Dino to slip into oblivion, busy as he was dealing with some present-day pains-in-the-ass—that was exactly the term he used at the end of a day of work when everyone had left the office and the phone would ring without a thought for the timing and Vittorio would answer irritably. "Don't worry about me, Vittorio," I would tell him. "No, it's always the same pains-in-the-ass, day and night!" From then on, he remembered him. Dino finally managed to climb over the trenches of the publishing houses and take his position with an Oscar in the cultural world and in miserable anthologies of trumpets, windbags, and trombones who continue blaring away with obscene determination. To give you an idea: There are volumes of *Meridiani* devoted to one ideological windbag from the left and not one devoted to Campana.

I can only be an outcast. It's not possible for someone like me not to be one. The motives are the same we have just spoken of. To boot, I don't shut my mouth; they would like to shut me up with their silence on my work because of my adolescent's "pseudo-political compromise." Just think that, in 1998, a "cultural worker" in my hometown of Legnago, with a forehead as hairy as that of his communist mates, wrote a letter to the newspaper *L'Arena di Verona* against my presence there, depicting me as a seventeen-year-old boss of the Italian Social Republic, when I had been exonerated and archived long back, in 1951. They're bent on intimidating me by not even writing about me negatively. If they did write, it would be obvious they were doing so because I am goading them, which is what I'm doing now, or because… They wouldn't dare: A lit matchstick of realization blinds them and keeps them from not bashing my work, so as to avoid total ridicule. They cannot be more abjectly filthy than this. Because right from their first fly-swatter scrawl, they realize that it's their bile possessing them, that their ashes are buried in anthologies and graveyards ministered by paid gravediggers. They have the flawed ambition of misfits with a lurid soul. For my part, I don't suffer from either jealousy or envy. I work for the poetry of other poets, and what little recognition I have gained has come with a lot of sweat. There is not a single big or small publisher who can boast of the honor of having rejected me. I never submitted any of my work; if anything, they have the dishonor of having relegated me into indifference. Barring your recent forceful initiative to present me to the critics, I can pretend that the rose manna of the publisher-whorehouses must come and discover me. Nor can anyone accuse me of mistaken ambition. I never asked nor ever ask for favors from anyone, and nobody ever reads my work at the poetry contests I don't take part in. At the 1967 Premio Viareggio, my first published work was submitted by Mondadori. The jury did not award the prize to *Sessions with My Analyst*, which stayed in the shortlist right to the end, because, at the time, they used to give the award to those digging in the communist coffers. I dare anyone, in spite of the false democratic appearances of the intelligentsia, to compare the award-winning book to mine, without any "ideological" bias. I won another prize in 1988, having submitted upon their invitation. I know that all those who are aware of their own meanness, in both the bloc of the elect and the bloc of the sheep, are not surprised when they find themselves in the explicit caption at the beginning of the volume *Paradigm*. In case nobody has read it, let me repeat it here:

> I'm condemned to look you in your little poet rodent eyes
> Destined to gnaw on your amanuensis identity.

If I hit, I also accept getting hit back. But there is a deep difference that sets us apart: I am generous, as are just a few others like me. I truly love and respect poetry. I'm honest, likable, and there's proof for it; they, generous in their barters, are stingy, false, jealous, envious, ugly mugs, and there's proof for it; all of them judged by time that sifts the sands, scraps the rotten parts, buries the offal, and shines with what little is left that's worthwhile.

I and my art don't need to hurry.

Roberto Bertoldo: Earlier, you were talking about Campana as a "true poet." I obviously agree, but is this enough to make him great? I judge him, precisely because of his canon, to be an imitator. All the while, I protect him and affirm the power of his poetry, which, however, in this sense, is the opposite of yours—more visionary than human.

Alfredo de Palchi: Fortunately, he is his own imitator. His is, at the end of the day, the only uncontrolled and yet crystal clear experience and thus, in his own way, controlled. It's the instinct of the visionary poet. Can you imagine lots of second-class bells imitating the great bell Campana? He is not a poet to be imitated. Comparing his poetry to mine, you say that his is the opposite of mine, which you say is more human. I hope it isn't. I prefer to have the fierce poetry of the gentle animal that has its own canon, i.e., instinct. If the poet is an artist, he possesses an animal's candor and canon.

Roberto Bertoldo: The American edition of *Paradigm* is the title of the book that collects all your poetry through 2009 and is taken from an Italian book of yours which first appeared in 2001. Can you explain this title?

Alfredo de Palchi: Yes, I'll explain it in just a minute. The 2001 book, despite a number of favorable reviews, went unnoticed and undistributed due to a lack of interest on the part of the publisher or the printing press—whatever. So let me get to the title's final enigma by telling you briefly about an event in which there was no other "animal." I'd been invited to read three poems at a conference on contemporary Italian poetry; on that day, I hadn't felt well since the early morning. However, a few days earlier, I had decided to avoid showing up at the venue so as not to have to administer to them the traumatic jolt I had in mind: not reading the poems listed in the program of events but rather the page I was going to write for the occasion. Why should I stir up the useless enmity of those useless people? In fact, on the following morning at eight o'clock, I get a phone call from them asking what had kept me at home. I didn't tell the original truth but the other truth, the easier one: I wasn't feeling well. Come today, they suggested, October 28. "All right," I answer, "I'll get a move on." In the theater, they're holding forth on poetic canons. During a break, I see some people I know, we say hello to each other. There are others I don't know, from Italy. Nobody introduces us, and I, a rogue and an arrogant snob when I need to be one, give them a wide berth. Later on, the moderator introduces me to the public. At the end of my brief reading, an endless string of versifiers started in. I listened, appalled. At the end of the conference, they ask me what special reason there is for the title of my collection, *Paradigm*. I take this unexpected opportunity to answer your question, reworking in a different way the sense of what I had planned to say then: "Today, I've listened to as much homespun poetry as you can listen to. *Paradigm* signifies quite simply an example for the so-called Italian poets, who should read me and imitate me." The moderator comments on my alleged modesty. "I agree, too much of it," I answer with a laugh. And I'm already enjoying that fact that, though curious, they're all avoiding me.

Roberto Bertoldo: What difference do you see between Italian authors in Italy and the much smaller number of Italian authors in America?

Alfredo de Palchi: To tell the truth, with my undiplomatic behavior, I teach a lesson of poetry to the world of cronyism of Italian poetry in Italy. The Sybil's voice inspires my lesson. It is said that the handful of Italian writers who live and work in the United States are derided and dismissed by the army of "poets" who live and die on paper in Italy; and this surely more ignorant than ridiculous army have styled themselves as superior to that mere handful. Quite probably it remains a rumor and nothing else. But still it requires the following clarification: the army of losers, having wrapped their foot cloths around their blah-blah-choked heads, too often prod the mere handful to get on with it and publish in our literary reviews and as books American versions of their attacks of brain fever, which still much too often end up as static cascades of dictionary words.

The army does not appreciate that the mere handful devote themselves, without asking for anything in exchange, to spreading Italian poetry; yet in spite of our passion and generosity in the face of humiliation, our poetry remains humiliated and has trouble making its mark on this continent, which tends to ignore foreign work. I've had no little experience of this through Chelsea Editions, and Luigi Fontanella has had his own experiences through his Gradiva Editions. But is it worthwhile persisting? Yes, undoubtedly yes, even though the army snorts at making any acknowledgment. I don't know what my colleagues in America think about this. But I, condescendingly, firmly reply that, if all goes well, most of the army come out even at the technical level, but with scarce poetic results, compared to the poetry of the handful, who have a wider knowledge of life. It's that the army has nothing to say since they have nothing to say, barricaded as they are in their own void. Poetry is true not when it's narrated or described in a void, but only if there is a real-life experience that appears in images leaping and skipping about on the page. Poetry is either poetry, or it is not. I confirm that most of the poetry that toes the line of the established canon or canons, and that poetry that toes the line of a pseudo avant-garde full of thick-headed nonsense, is as gruesome as an abortion; or, to be less cruel, I say it ends up with the same result: failure. From this you can understand that I, although I slap and kick, love and defend the poetry of both blocs—the elect and the herd. It all depends. But I am aware of my failed attacks against the windmills; they are defeats that all the more urge me to appeal to the justice of poetry also in the name of those who, on the sidelines, neither bleat out nor make an outcry, and let nothingness grow larger. A few rare persons will help. An honest critic here and there. While we wait, I democratically urge the army of extinguished windmills to stop fanning hot air about and limit the annihilation of forests.

Roberto Bertoldo: Okay, dear Alfredo, our interview is at an end. I'll let you speak the last word.

Alfredo de Palchi: I'm grateful to you for this interview. It's got quite a lot of different thoughts in it, insights, legitimate overstatements, episodes of my life without bathos. I'm not joking when I repeat that my lesson is absolutely valid for the alleged establishment poets and those of the homespun style. As soon as they have angrily and enviously finished reading the interview and the critical essays here, I suggest they open themselves up to the real, following the example—my *Paradigm*—even if they do it on the sly and cursing me.

Afterword

John Taylor

In the landscape that consists of American poetry and the foreign verse available in translation, the originality and independence of Alfredo de Palchi have long been conspicuous. As an Italian poet who has lived in the United States for more than fifty years, who continues to write exclusively in Italian, yet whose work has been extensively translated ever since *Sessions with My Analyst* and especially *The Scorpion's Dark Dance*, *Anonymous Constellation*, and *Addictive Aversions*, de Palchi stands out because of his terse, tense verse wrought out of syntactic boldness, semantic leaps (indeed recalling Joseph Brodsky's notion of poetry "accelerating thought"), unsentimental self-scrutiny, and tonalities ranging from sarcasm to erotic glorification. His subject matter draws on his own experiences, especially in his early poems evoking his impoverished, fatherless childhood, his suffering during the Second World War, and his unjust postwar incarceration. In his later verse, he leaves this grim wartime past behind, scrutinizes man-woman relationships, exalts sexual pleasure, and turns toward science, notably biology and geology, in an effort to cast light on the bleakness of the human condition. The at once precise and idiosyncratic way that science is brought to bear on his dark view of human behavior and, more generally, of the human condition alone distinguishes him from most contemporary poets in the United States and Europe. The particularities of his kaleidoscopic or—if I may venture the analogy—"cubist" poetics set him apart. He has forged a short poetic form that juxtaposes bits of thoughts, feelings, or sense impressions; the edges are purposely left raw and rugged.[1]

NOTES

1. This afterword is part of John Taylor's essay in Alfredo de Palchi, *Paradigm: Selected and New Poems 1947–2009*, edited by John Taylor, various translators. New York: Chelsea Editions, 2013. Taylor is an American writer, critic, and translator who lives in France. His most recent translations of de Palchi's poetry include: *The Aesthetics of Equilibrium* (Xenos Books/Chelsea Editions, 2019), *At An Hour's Sleep From Here* (The Bitter Oleander Press, 2020), and *Nihil* (Xenos Books, 2017).

Bibliography

Adorno, Theodor W. *Aesthetic Theory*, edited by Gretel Adorno and Rolf Tiedemann, translated by Robert Hullot-Kentor. London, New York: Continuum, 2002.

Anceschi, Luciano. *Autonomia ed eteronomia dell'arte*. Milan: Garzanti, [1959] 1992.

Benjamin, Walter. *The Work of Art in the Age of Mechanical Reproduction*. In: *Illuminations*, edited by Hannah Arendt, translated by Harry Zohn, from the 1935 essay. New York: Schocken Books, 1969.

Berardinelli, Alfonso. "Post-ermetismo e sperimentazione da Sereni a Pasolini." In *La Cultura del 900*, edited by Alfonso Berardinelli and Costanzo Di Girolamo. Milan: Mondadori, 1981.

———. *Casi critici. Dal postmoderno alla mutazione*. Macerata, Italy: Quodlibet, 2012.

Bertoldo, Roberto. "Leggere Alfredo de Palchi," *Scritti sulla poesia di Alfredo de Palchi*, edited by Roberto Bertoldo. Turin, Italy: I quaderni di Hebenon, 2000.

———. "Intervista ad Alfredo de Palchi." In *Alfredo de Palchi. La potenza della poesia*, edited by Roberto Bertoldo. Alessandria, Italy: Edizioni dell'Orso, 2008.

Bonaffini, Luigi, and Joseph Perricone, eds. *Poets of the Italian Diaspora: A Bilingual Anthology*. New York: Fordham University Press, 2013.

Borghi, Claudio. https://lombradelleparole.wordpress.com/2016/11/01/pier-luigi-bacchinipoesie-scelte-con-una-poetry-dedicata-di-claudio-borghi-un-suo-appuntocritico-e-un-commento-impolitico-di-giorgio-linguaglossa/comment-page-1/#comment-15966 (accessed November 1, 2016).

Carravetta, Peter. "Introduzione." In *Poesaggio: poeti italiani d'America*, edited by Peter Carravetta and Paolo Valesio. Quinto di Treviso, Italy: Pagus, 1993.

de Palchi, Alfredo. *Sessioni con l'analista*. Milan: Mondadori, 1967.

———. *Sessions with My Analyst*, translated by I. L. Salomon. New York: October House, 1970.

———. *Mutazioni*. Udine: Campanotto, 1988.

——. *The Scorpion's Dark Dance / La buia danza di scorpione*, translated by Sonia Raiziss. Riverside, CA: Xenos Books, 1993.

——. *Anonymous Constellation / Costellazione anonima*, translated by Santa Raiziss. Riverside, CA: Xenos Books, 1997.

——. *Costellazione anonima*. Marina di Minturno, Italy: Caramanica, 1998.

——. *Addictive Aversions / Le viziose avversioni*, translated by Sonia Raiziss and others. Riverside, CA: Xenos Books, 1999.

——. *Paradigma*. Marina di Minturno, Italy: Caramanica, 2001.

——. *Paradigma: Tutte le poesie 1947–2005*. Milan: Mimesis / Hebenon, 2006.

——. *Dates and Fevers of Anguish*, translated by Luigi Bonaffini and Michael Palma. Stony Brook, NY: Gradiva Publications, 2006.

——. *Contro la mia morte*. Padua, Italy: Libreria Padovana Editrice, 2007.

——. *Foemina Tellus*. Novi Ligure, Italy: Edizioni Joker, 2010.

——. *Paradigm: Selected and New Poems 1947–2009*, edited by John Taylor, various translators. New York: Chelsea Editions, 2013.

——. *Nihil*. Azzate, Italy: Stampa2009, 2016.

——. *Nihil*, translated by John Taylor. Las Cruces, NM: Xenos Books, 2017.

——. *Estetica dell'equilibrio*. Milan: Mimesis / Hebenon, 2017.

Derrida, Jacques. *Speech and Phenomena*, translated by David B. Allison. Evanston, IL: Northwestern University Press, 1973.

——. *Writing and Difference*, translated by Alan Bass. Chicago: The University of Chicago Press, 1978.

——. *Of Grammatology*, translated by Gayatri Chakavorty Spivak. Baltimore, MD: Johns Hopkins University Press, 1997.

Erba, Luciano. "Alfredo de Palchi: Gentile animale braccato." In *Almanacco dello Specchio*, 11. Milan: Mondadori, 1983.

Ferraris, Maurizio. *Emergenze*. Turin, Italy: Einaudi, 2016.

Fontanella, Luigi, ed. *Una vita scommessa in poesia: Omaggio ad Alfredo de Palchi. A Life Gambled in Poetry: Homage to Alfredo de Palchi*. New York: Gradiva Publications, 2011.

——. *La parola transfuga*. Florence: Cadmo, 2003; in English as *Migrating Words: Italian Writers in the United States*. New York: Bordighera Press, 2012.

Freud, Sigmund. "The Acquisition and Control of Fire." In *Freud's Complete Works 1890–1939*, http://staferla.free.fr/Freud/Freud%20complete%20Works.pdf (accessed June 1, 2016).

——. *Writings on Art and Literature*. Stanford, CA: Stanford University Press, 1997.

——. *On Metapsychology: The Theory of Psychoanalysis*. London: Penguin, 1991.

Jakobson, Roman. *Language in Literature*, edited by Krystyna Pomorska and Stephen Rudy. Cambridge, MA; London: The Belknap Press of Harvard University Press, 1987.

Jung, Carl Gustav. *Symbols of Transformation*, translated by R. F. C. Hull. Princeton, NJ: Princeton University Press, 1956.

Lacan, Jacques. *Le séminaire, Livre XI. Les quatre concepts fondamentaux de la psychanalyse*. Paris: Seuil, 1964.

————. *The Seminar, Book II. The Ego in Freud's Theory and in the Technique of Psychoanalysis, 1954–1955*, edited by Jacques-Alain Miller, translated by Sylvana Tomaselli. New York: W.W. Norton, 1988.

————. "The Direction of the Treatment and the Principles of Its Power." In *Écrits: The First Complete Edition in English*, translated by Bruce Fink. New York: W.W. Norton, 2006.

Lecomte, Mia. *Di un poetico altrove. Poesia transnazionale italofona (1960–2016)*. Florence: Franco Cesati Editore, 2018.

Linguaglossa, Giorgio, ed. *Come è finita la guerra di Troia non ricordo*. Rome: Progetto Cultura, 2016.

Miller, Jacques-Alain. *Paradigms of Jouissance*, translated by Jorge Jauregui, http://www.lacan.com/frameXVII2.htm (accessed June 1, 2016).

Ramat, Silvio. "Sessioni con l'analista." In *La Fiera Letteraria*, July 27, 1967.

Tamburri, Anthony Julian. *Un biculturalismo negato. La letteratura "italiana" negli Stati Uniti*. Florence: Franco Cesati Editore, 2018.

Terzi, Roberto. *Il soggetto Me l'al di là del significato: tra Heidegger e Lacan*. Milan: Noema, 2013.

Valesio, Paolo. "I fuochi della tribù." In *Poesaggio: poeti italiani d'America*, edited by Peter Carravetta and Paolo Valesio. Quinto di Treviso, Italy: Pagus, 1993.

Vettori, Alessandro. "Introduction." In *Anonymous Constellation*, by Alfredo de Palchi. Riverside, CA: Xenos Books, 1997.

Zagaroli, Antonella. "Alfredo de Palchi, Alcuni Paradigmi dell'Opera Poetica." In *Una vita scommessa in poesia: Omaggio ad Alfredo de Palchi. A Life Gambled in Poetry: Homage to Alfredo de Palchi*, edited by Luigi Fontanella. New York: Gradiva Publications, 2011.

Zanzotto, Andrea. *Motivation for Awarding the 1988 City of San Vito al Tagliamento Poetry Prize Speech*. July 30, 1988.

Index

About the Author

Giorgio Linguaglossa is a critic, author, and poet. He was born in Istanbul in 1949 and lives in Rome. Linguaglossa published his first poetic work, *Uccelli* (Rome: Edizioni Scettro del Re) in 1992 and has published seven collections of poetry to date. From 1992 to 2005, he directed the poetry series of Edizioni Scettro del Re di Roma. In 1993, Linguaglossa founded the quarterly magazine *Poiesis*. He has written extensively on contemporary Italian poetry, edited critical presentations of numerous Italian poets, and collaborates as a critic with the literature magazines *Polimnia*, *Hebenon*, *Altroverso*, and *Capoverso*. In 2014, Linguaglossa founded the blog lombradelleparole. wordpress.com. His poems have been translated into Spanish, English, and Bulgarian.

ABOUT THE TRANSLATOR

Steven Grieco-Rathgeb is a Swiss-born poet and translator who writes in Italian and English. In 2015, he translated Giorgio Linguaglossa's *Three Stills in the Frame: Selected Poems, 1986–2014*, and, in 2016, Roberto Bertoldo's *Victim's Cram: Selected Poems*, both for Chelsea Editions.